Product Design 6

Product Design 6

Tucker Viemeister

LIBRARY OF APPLIED DESIGN

An Imprint of
PBC International, Inc.

Distributor to the book trade in the United States and Canada
Rizzoli International Publications Inc.
300 Park Avenue South
New York, NY 10010

Distributor to the art trade in the United States and Canada
PBC International, Inc.
One School Street
Glen Cove, NY 11542
1-800-527-2826
Fax 516-676-2738

Distributor throughout the rest of the world
Hearst Books International
1350 Avenue of the Americas
New York, NY 10019

ISBN 0-86636-280-0 ✓
ISSN 1072-4494

CAVEAT– Information in this text is believed accurate, and will pose no problem for the student or
casual reader. However, the author was often constrained by information contained in signed
release forms, information that could have been in error or not included at all. Any misinformation
(or lack of information) is the result of failure in these attestations. The author has done whatever
is possible to insure accuracy.

Color separation, printing and binding by
Toppan Printing Co., (H.K.) Ltd.
Printed in China

10 9 8 7 6 5 4 3 2 1

Dedicated to

Read Viemeister *(1922–1993)*

The most talented designer (and Dad) I ever knew!

Table of contents

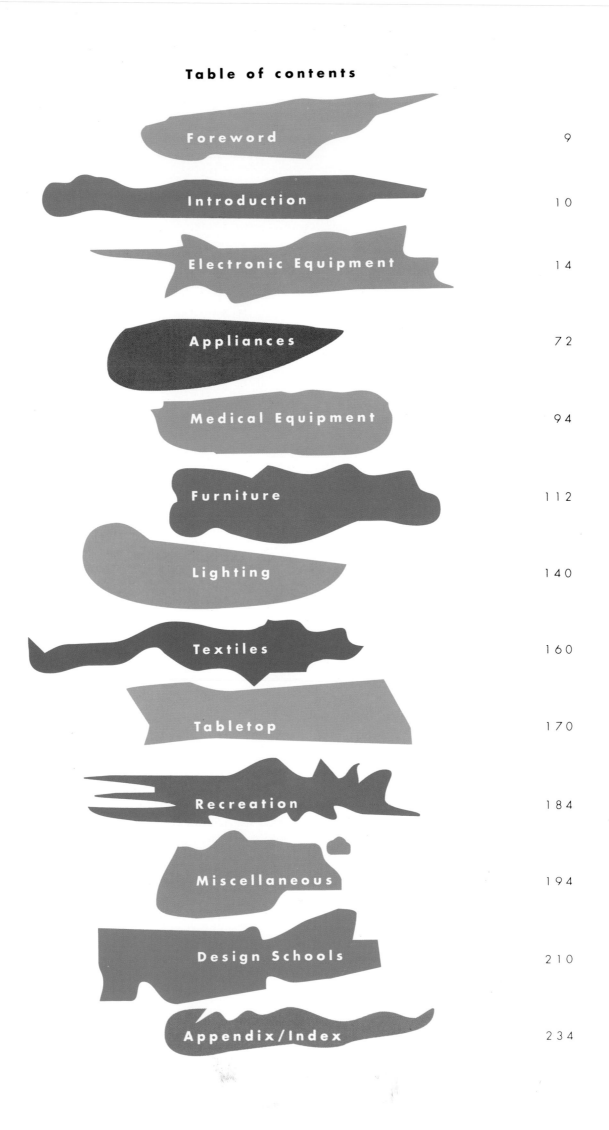

Dianne H. Pilgrim

Director, Cooper-Hewitt Museum, the Smithsonian Institution's National Museum of Design

Design is not just a way of describing the appearance of an object, a styling tool, or a method of problem-solving; it is a complex thought process. When we consider design in this light it becomes obvious that design is something very powerful that affects all parts of our lives, both large and small, personal and global.

The products of design give us the potential to live full and satisfying lives. Imagine life without the most basic designed necessities for eating, sleeping, commuting or playing. From silverware to alarm clocks to subway cars and hockey sticks, our lives are dictated by the products of design. For their practical functions as well as their role in cultural identities, designed objects have significant power in our lives.

Nearing the end of the twentieth century, we have begun to view design with a new and different emphasis. "We" has come to mean the consumer, the designer, and the manufacturer. The voice of the consumer has grown more forceful in regard to design. Designers and manufacturers have begun to respond to our real needs. The word "responsibility" (which goes hand in hand with power) figures more prominently in the designer's and manufacturer's vocabularies. Prompted by federal legislation (like the Americans with Disabilities Act), designers and manufacturers are beginning to think more about access and function as equal partners with aesthetics and styling. The power of design works both ways.

As the director of the National Museum of Design, I applaud the designers and manufacturers represented in *Product Design 6*. Their concepts and products are part of the chronicle of late twentieth-century problem-solving and clearly illustrate the way design figures into every aspect of our lives. The pages that follow are a testament to the extraordinary power and influence design brings to our world.

Schecter Lee

Tucker Viemeister

Vice President, Smart Design Inc.

L ike the people who lived during the Dark Ages, we can't help thinking that life has always been like it is today. Everything seems pretty normal because we live in a time when historic changes—magnificent and catastrophic alike—happen so frequently that we don't pay much attention at all. But look around, the Modern era is over and Post-Modernism, Communism and the Cold War are finished. The Information Age is in full swing and almost everything is different from the way it was only a few years ago.

When the Roman Empire and the Industrial Revolution radically altered community and commercial structures, people had to respond to the upheaval. Now we don't even pause before we flip to another channel. We don't realize that we use the telephone more times a day than we use a fork, or that kids watch 8,000 murders on TV by the time they're eight years old, anymore than we remember that women got the right to vote in the USA *only* 70 years ago or that astronauts stood on the moon *more* than 20 years ago.

We're faced with a *transparent revolution* that's changing all our lives. Either people are doing an incredibly good job of integrating all this change into their lives or, more likely, it's building up like puss in a boil. Our social structure can't take much more "progress" before it blows. All you have to do is look at the disparity between the "have's" and the "have not's," or worse, between the "know's" and the "dunno's."

Technology was supposed to be our saviour, but there are real questions about its ability to overcome the twin threats of over-population and ecological disaster before they overtake us. On a personal level, people are wondering what they're going to do when robots take over their jobs. And what's a designer like me going to do when my computer is smarter than I am?

The trend in technology has been from <u>mechanical</u> to <u>chemical</u> to <u>electronic</u> and now it's moving rapidly toward <u>biological</u>. The shift from motors to computers has enabled technology to become increasingly sophisticated and invisible, enabling it to sneak into our lives without us noticing. We are moving away from gadgets and gizmos and toward imbedding the technology deep inside the product so that a more sensual and intuitive relationship is possible between the artifact and the user. Our tools are becoming more flexible and more responsive to the user—more like pets than appliances. Someday in the future, they may even come to life—we'll have to be careful so we don't end up in some real-life Jurassic Park nightmare.

Bike basket

Pool chair with Holt & Krohn

Lisa Krohn's answering machine

Sardine light with Krohn

Industrial designers have the tools <u>and</u> the opportunity to make the world a better place if they are willing to accept the responsibility. Design is not like smearing jam on toast. Designers must do more than simply interpret technology and make it useful and pretty. Scientists define intelligence as the ability to "capture and apply information" but I call that design and that is exactly what we have to do.

The world has changed since Loewy, Vassos and the rest of those pioneers gave birth to our profession. Shifting from "visionaries" to "problem solvers," design continuously de-evolved to meet the increasingly narrow requirements of industry. Today, the design profession is stalled. Design has not become the buzzword of the '90s as *Business Week* predicted three years ago, and the prospects are not bright.

What is preventing the profession from doing all that it can? William Drenttel, president of Drenttel Doyle, points to the "dumb designer syndrome." He believes the phenomenon stems from "the desire to hide behind the right side of the brain. This (syndrome), in some cases, flows directly from the historically inferior position designers hold in many worlds. Magazine art directors seldom have the power of editors... and corporate art directors are usually in staff positions without line responsibility."

Product designers find themselves acting as pimps for industry, dressing up products to attract consumers. Some think of themselves more like prostitutes, stimulating businesses for cash. Sensitivity to environmental and social concerns is leading young designers (who are less dependent on the material wealth that our economy runs on) to see themselves as pushers, supplying the habits of the junkie consumer. Sure, design gives industry a competitive edge, but doesn't it also have a higher calling?

What happened to our profession? Designers were always the optimists. For the 1939 World's Fair, Norman Bel Geddes created *Futurama* and Henry Dreyfuss built *Democracity*. Designers transformed new materials and new inventions into things people wanted—streamlined cars, modern highways, inspiring buildings, turbo-charged appliances, and visionary graphics. They created models for how things could be; everything was open for improvement; progress was around every corner. Their visions of utopia drove our economy through World War II and into the late '60s. But now there are only a few optimists left—people like Bill Stumpf, Philippe Starck, and Maya Lin. Who would have thought that just when science and technology are delivering us to the threshold of a more realist utopia, we would be stuck with too many pessimistic and short-sighted designers.

B-52 Swing Speaker

Platinum pen

Markuse weather vane

Jaws of Time sundial

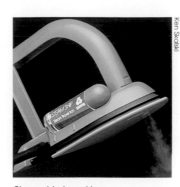

Steamship travel iron

Serengeti sunglasses

Maybe designers are no different from all the other people who feel powerless when they are confronted by all our world's BIG problems. I hope not because I still believe that design is the only responsible way to make a difference. Technology, ecology and society are demanding a new kind of designer—one who knows when to *do* or *undo* or even *not do*.

Design is the essence of empowerment. In the broadest sense, design is how human beings take charge of their own lives and how they figure out how to live together. It is much more than a marketing strategy for styling products. It is basic to human fulfillment. It recognizes cultural differences as a valuable resource and it seeks to make the most of them. It is also one hell of a tool for business and government. Democracy is the rule—design is the tool.

But why does American society find it so hard to support something as fundamentally good as design?

The problem is that the general public doesn't see design the way designers do. They see design as style. They think that a lot of it is ugly and usually bad. Not only that, they think it usually gets in the way and it's expensive. Unfortunately, they're right. They like "the ugly and ordinary" stuff Robert Venturi and Denies Scott Brown found in *Learning from Las Vegas*.

It seems like the public and designers have gone separate ways. So when we preach the need for *even more* design, they think we must be *mad!* They can't imagine how anyone can think that more stupid designer junk will improve their lives and help them prosper. How can a few designers possibly do that?

Designers don't need government programs, we need national involvement. Designers need to show people how design can improve the quality of their lives and how objects shape our culture and define our lives. We have to teach everyone from kids to CEOs how to create, evaluate and exploit design. We have to demonstrate and quantify the economic benefits of design. People have to believe that when design is an integral part of any activity, it improves that activity. And we have to prove it by making products better—not simply products that appeal to consumers but products that work better, feel better, sound better, and cost less too!

In the ideal world, business and government are servants of design. That's not to say that designers become the priests at the top of the pyramid. That wouldn't be smart or fair. Design is choice and consequences. To make any practical advances, design thinking has to be incorporated into our daily lives. We have to get everyone thinking ahead, everyone being sympathetic to the needs and desires of others, everyone doing the best they can—everyone designing!

Copco salad servers

Chopper and bowl

Scientific apparatus

My Frame picture frame

Black & Decker toaster

Lassie Come Home doghouse

This collection is not meant to be an objective selection of the best and most important products of 1992. It is simply my personal selection from all the pictures that people sent me. Lots of these things I'd never seen before and some of these things we all know. Some things are perfect and some *anyone* could improve. In short, this book is made up of the things that struck me as interesting—interesting to look at, maybe a novel approach, maybe a nice picture, or a cool combination of materials or a beautiful form. (To help you understand my perspective, I have illustrated this intro-duction with photographs of objects that I've designed on my own or as a partner at Smart Design.)

We have consciously limited the scope of this book to just product design (after all, that is the name!). But industrial designers design other things too, like exhibits, signage, graphics and packaging. Understanding good design is like understanding numbers—once you figure them out you can count apples or figure out that $E=mc^2$.

Hopefully, the images in this book will help bridge the gap between "design" artifacts that exist solely for their stylish aesthetics and "functional" artifacts that people use or consume in their everyday life. This bridge between these two types of artifacts is important because in order to make truly amazing products, designers must create something that they like as well as something that other people like and can use. As Jack Cottrell, president of Details, puts it, "it's the job of the designer to push."

Lastly, I need to thank the people at PBC, especially Kevin Clark (who convinced me that doing this book would be worth all the work), Susan Kapsis (who guided the editorial process), Debra Harding (who cataloged and wrote all the captions), Garrett Schuh (who laid out the book) and Joanne Caggiano (who tracked down and collected all the submissions). Special thanks to David Hales, my associate at Smart and intellectual sparring partner, who sharpened up the ideas while he corrected my spelling. The real heroes of this book are all the designers represented here who couldn't "leave well enough alone," and who used their talent, insights and intellect to make the impossible possible, and used their imagination to make theirs and our dreams come true.

For me, this book will be a success if it inspires people to imagine a better future. These images represent only the tip of the iceberg—design is everywhere—and without it, what's the point?

Oxo *Good Grips*

Corkscrew

Birdhouse for Koizumi

Cars used to be like the Olympics for a lot of designers, but since the early 1980s electronic products have been the most prized commissions. There's something about the mix of science, competition, and money that historically attracts industrial designers.

In the not-too-distant future, advancements in technology are going to make this category obsolete. Computer technology will be so deeply imbedded in products that we'd never think of as electronic. Traditionally "dumb" products will become "smart" products and the product form will no longer be distinct from the user interface.

Electronic Equipment

Product

777 Flight Deck

Flight deck of twin-engine airplane accommodates 2 pilots
and 2 observers.

Designer

777 Flight Deck

Design Team

Manufacturer

The Boeing Airplane

Company

Photographer

The Boeing Airplane

Company

Product

**Series 900 Systems and
Servers**

Enclosures mate mechanically
and electronically to provide
VMEbus based array.

Designers

**Tom Shoda, industrial
designer; John Toor,
mechanical designer—
Palo Alto Industrial Design
Group, Inc.**

Manufacturer

**Motorola Inc., Motorola
Computer Group**

Photographer

Motorola

Product

**Open Office Enclosure
Family**

Three sizes accept variety of
modular equipment.

Designers

Robert Hanson

Meg Hetfield

Manufacturer

Digital Equipment Corp.

Photographer

Ed Horrigan

Product

Storage Express

Back up server for local
area networks.

Designer

**Rob Dillon,
Sohrab Vossoughi—
ZIBA Design Team**

Manufacturer

Intel Corporation

Photographer

Michael Jones

Product

Computer Peripherals

Line of computer peripherals
can be used independantly or
stacked in any combination.

Designers

Edward Cruz,

Barry Sween,

Vince Razo,

Terron Newman—

S.G. Hauser Associates, Inc.

Manufacturer

BlackCurrant Technologies

Photographer

Terry Sutherland

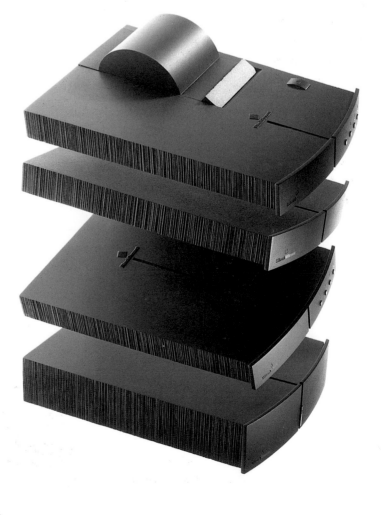

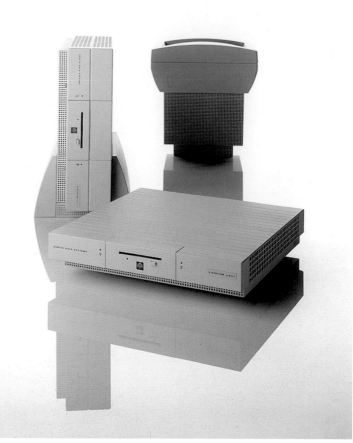

Product

CL2000 Disk Array

Data storage subsystem
allows repair and replace-
ment without system shut-down.

Designers

Mark Bates

Corporate Design Staff

Manufacturer

Data General

Photographer

Jose' Ramos, Data

General

Product

Z-System

Computer system with sym-
metrical interface areas for
right and left hand access.

Designers

Hartmut Esslinger,

Dan Harden—

frogdesign inc.

Manufacturer

Zenith Data Systems

Photographer

Mario Parnell

Product

The ATIC Computer

Terminal

Monochrome terminal reduces
product cost and OEM
order fulfillment time.

Designers

Edward Cruz,

David Weir,

Vince Razo,

David Hoard—

S.G. Hauser Associates, Inc.

Manufacturer

LINK Technologies, Inc.

Photographer

Terry Sutherland

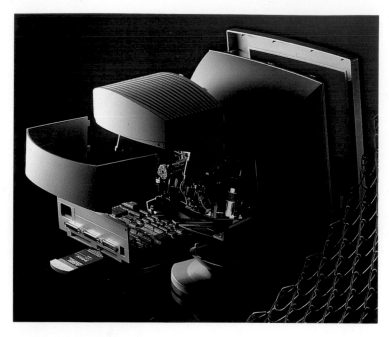

Product

The ATIC Computer Terminal
Shows interior elements
and demonstrates the
ease of production.
Designers
Edward Cruz,
David Weir,
Vince Razo,
David Hoard—
S.G. Hauser Associates, Inc.
Photographer
Terry Sutherland

Product

Apple Quadra 800
Computer designed for publishing,
design and multimedia industries.
Designers
Ken Wood, project manager,
industrial designer;
Gil Wong, Matt Barthelemy,
industrial design;
Robert Brunner, manager;
Ray Riley, project manager—
Apple Industrial Design
Manufacturer
Apple Computer, Inc.
Photographer
Rick English

Product

Apple 14" Color Monitor
Low cost color monitor inte-
grates tilt-swivel and
up-front controls.
Designers
Mark Biasotti, IDEO
Product Development;
Jim Stewart, Apple Computer
Manufacturer
Apple Computer, Inc.
Photographer
Miles Keep

Product
**NCR System
3225/3230/3333**
Entry level products for family of high-
end general purpose computers.
Designers
**Werner Stephan,
industrial designer
Graham Marshall
Robert Kelley
Brian Jablonski**
Manufacturer
NCR Corporation
Photographer
Alexander, Glass, Ingersol Inc.

Product
ICI et Maintenant
Interactive displaying
computer.
Designer
Frechin et Bureaux
Manufacturer
Federation Francaise
Destravaux Public
Photographer
Malfada Minette

Product

HP TestBook

PC based automotive service tool with repair information and diagnostic capability.

Designers

Gil Lemke

Dave Skinner

Manufacturer

Hewlett-Packard Company, Integrated Systems Division

Photographer

Geoffrey Nelson

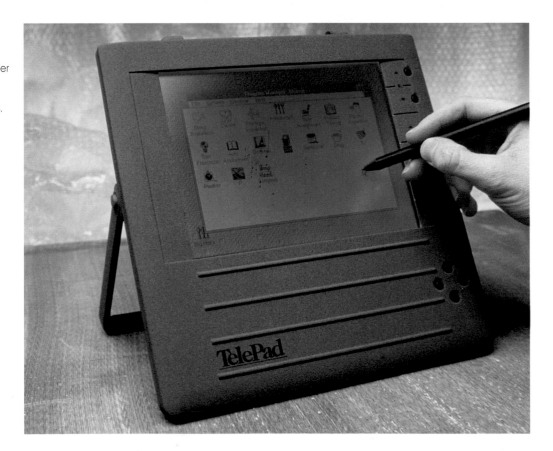

Product

TelePad SL

Portable pen-based computer with pen, keyboard, and communications capabilities.

Designers

Michael Barry,

Sue Brassil,

Mike Wise,

Ben Thomas—GVO Inc.

Manufacturer

TelePad Corporation, Reston, VA

Photographer

GVO Inc.

Product

PowerBook DUO System

Portable/desktop computer
system eliminates file synchro-
nization problems.

Designers

Gavin Ivester,

Jay Meschter,

Lawrence Lam—

Apple Industrial Design

Robert Riccomini,

Matt Herron —

Apple Product Design

Manufacturer

Apple Computer, Inc.

Photographer

Rick English

Product

Grid Convertible

Four-bar hinging mechanism
allows dual use as pen com-
puter/portable laptop.

Designers

Mark Biasotti, IDEO
Product Development;
Jack Daley, Grid Systems

Manufacturer

Grid Systems

Photographer

Miles Keep

Product

Apple PowerBook 100

Portable computer with
ergonomic keyboard/palm
rest and built-in trackball.

Designers

Ken Wood, project manager,
industrial designer; Matt
Barthelemy, industrial design;
Jeff Smith, design principal;
Robert Brunner, manager—
Apple Industrial Design

Manufacturer

Apple Computer, Inc.

Photographer

Rick English

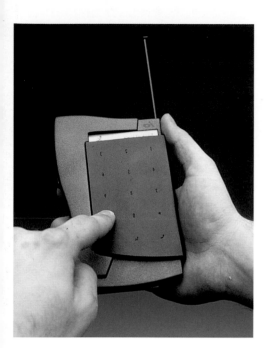  

Product

i/o Personal Digital

Assistant

Hand-held computer integrates touch technology and voice communications.

Designers

Michael Barry,

Shawn Hanna,

Jay Wilson—GVO Inc.

Manufacturer

Concept

Photographer

GVO Inc.

Product

PIC System

Personal information and

communication system.

Designers

Henry Chin,

Sohrab Vossoughi—

ZIBA Design Team

Manufacturer

General Magic Corporation

Photographer

Michael Jones

Product

HP ScanJet IIc Scanner

Scans color or monochrome

images and text.

Designers

Mo Khovaylo

Jim Dow

Manufacturer

Hewlett-Packard Company

Photographer

Jonathan Mankin

Product
GPX 1150 Printer
Electrophotographic printer
can image cut sheet and
fan folded paper.
Designer
Jay Wilson
Manufacturer
Toray, Japan
Photographer
Mark Gottlieb

Product
**Apple LaserWriter Pro
600/630 Series**
High performance, high
volume laser printer.
Designers
**Ken Wood, project manager,
industrial designer;
Jeff Smith, design principal,
Robert Brunner, manager,
Jim Stewart, Grant Ross—
Apple Industrial Design**
Manufacturer
Apple Computer, Inc.
Photographer
Rick English

Product

8050 Magnetic Card
Reader

Used in schools/test
oriented applications.

Designer

Joe Ricchio

Manufacturer

Scantron

Photographer

Joe Atlas,
Atlas Photography

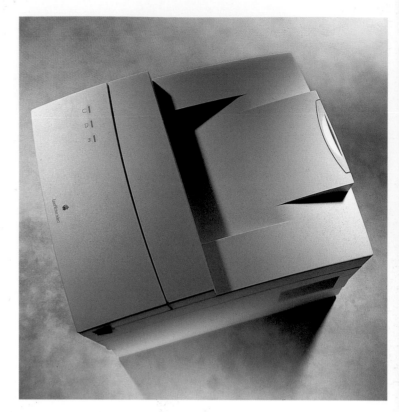

Product

Laserwriter Select

Three hundred dpi laser printer.

Designers

Mike Nutall, Nick Top—

IDEO Product Development

Jim Stewart, Apple Computer

Manufacturer

Apple Computer

Photographer

Rick English

Product

Fargo Label Printer

Prints labels of variety of

sizes and layouts.

Designers

Eric Mueller

Jim Luther

Manufacturer

Fargo Electronics, Inc.

Photographer

Fargo Electronics, Inc.

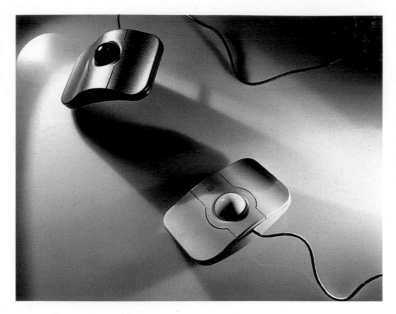

Product
Costar Stingray
Trackball with oversized buttons.
Designer
Paul Bradley
Manufacturer
Costar Corporatioı.
Photographer
Geoffrey Nelson

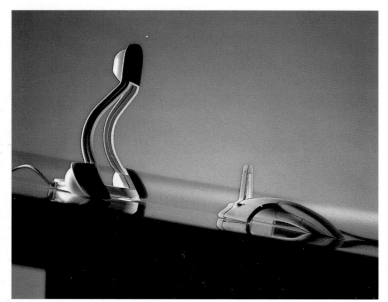

Product
Logitech 3-D Mouse
Five-button pointing device
inputs 3-D spatial information
using ultrasonics.
Designers
Paul Bradley
Lawrence Lam
Manufacturer
Logitech
Photographer
Rick English

Product
Alps OEM Mouse
Mouse with 4-inch interface
radius fits comfortably
in cupped hand.
Designers
Ken Wood, Max Yoshimoto,
industrial designers;
Gerard Fubershaw,
design principal
Manufacturer
Apls OEM Group
Photographer
Rick English

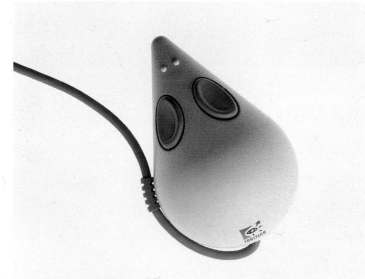

Product
kidz mouse
Computer mouse
designed for children.
Designers
Tino Melzer, Dan Harden—
frogdesign inc.
Manufacturer
Logitech
Photographer
frogdesign inc.

Product

PalmMouse

Wireless pointing device
designed to be worn on hand
while operating computer.

Designer

Donald Carr

Manufacturer

NCR Corporation

Photographer

Alexander, Glass, Ingersol Inc.

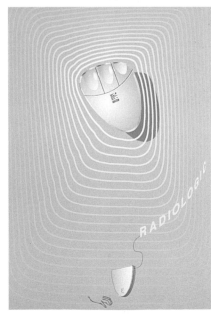

Product

Mouseman Cordless

Ball placement between index
finger and thumb increases
hand-eye coordination.

Designer

Montgomery/Pfeifer, Inc.

Manufacturer

Logitech

Photographer

Dietmar Henneka

Product

Apple Adjustable Keyboard

Split alphanumeric keyboard
with detatchable palm rests.

Designer

**Ray Riley, Apple Industrial
Design; Stephen Peart,
Vent Design; David Shen,
Apple Computer**

Manufacturer

Apple Computer

Photographer

Rick English

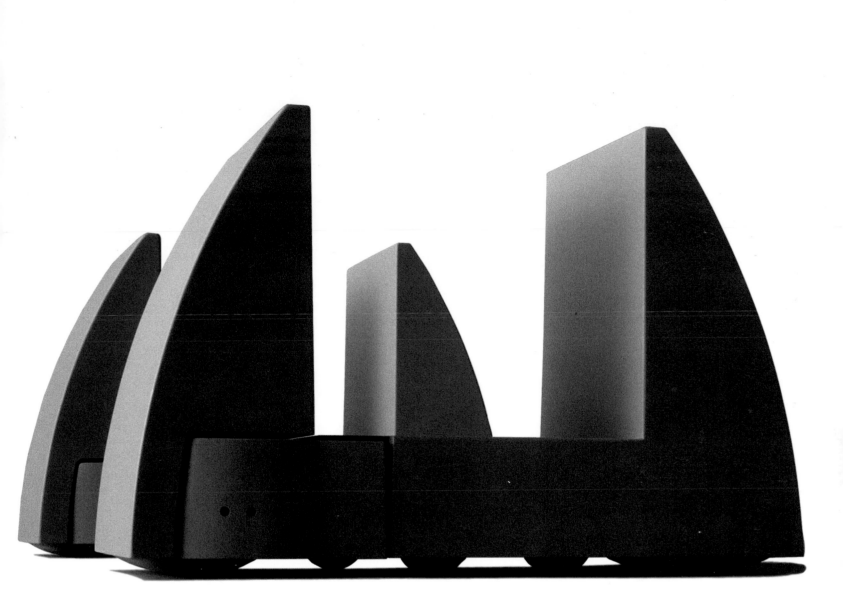

Product

Processor Support

Accommodates large number of processor types in simple, inexpensive way.

Designers

Naoto Fukasawa, Tim Brown, industrial design; Paul Howard, mechanical engineering

Manufactrurer

Details

Photographer

Charles Kemper

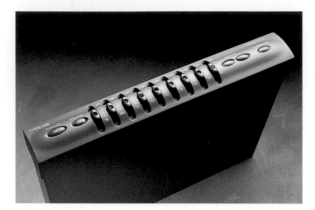

Product

Car Audio Equalizer

Lighted switches display and

adjust sound levels.

Designer

Mark Dziersk,

Group Four Design

Manufacturer

Audiovax

Photographer

Rick Whittey

Product

AD-1 Series Audio

Amplifier System

Audio amplifiers featuring

front panels inlaid with

gold plated ornaments.

Designer

Fumikazu Masuda

Manufacturer

Audio Devices Inc.

Photographer

Kiyoshi Teruuchi

Product

Preview Camera

Compact camera. Rotating
color LCD screen for viewfind-
ing and image assessment.

Designer

Stuart Harvey Lee

Manufacturer

***Concept* for Saurus Inc.,
Interaction Consultants,
Tokyo**

Photographer

Stuart Harvey Lee

Product

Snap Video Camera NV-CS1

Automatic camera/recorder; self-timer and one-touch tele-wide.

Designers

Seiichi Watanabe

Mitsuo Takanaga

Manufacturer

Matsushita Electric Industrial Co., Ltd.

Photographer

Matsushita Electric Industrial Co., Ltd.

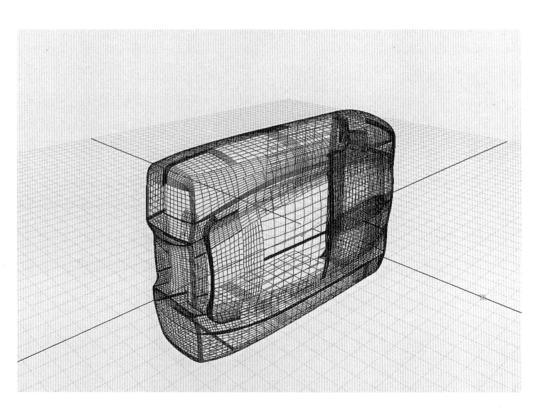

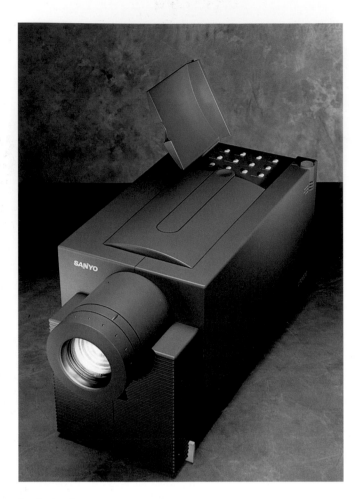

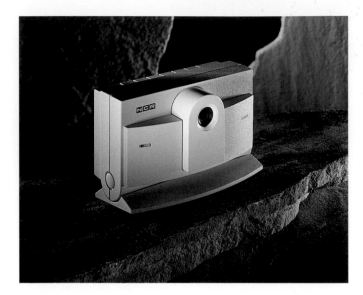

Product

™Telemedia Video Camera

Facilitates video-conferencing,

still frame image capture.

Designers

John Caldwell,

Robert Kelley,

Brian Jablonski—

NCR Consulting Design Group

Manufacturer

NCR Corporation

Photographer

Alexander, Glass, Ingersol Inc.

Product

LP 2000

High resolution LCD video pro-

jector for television or

video images.

Designers

Chris Alviar,

Sohrab Vossoughi—

ZIBA Design Team

Manufacturer

Sanyo Electronic

Corporation

Photographer

Michael Jones

Product

KP-41 EER96

Videoscope ® big screen TV with

inset freeze, picture/audio swap.

Designer

Sony Design Center

Manufacturer

Sony Corporation

Photographer

Sony Corporation

Products

Panasonic TH-21VT2

Panasonic TH-8VT1

Portable audio/video system combining VCR and television. Various screen sizes available.

Designer

Matshushi Kotobuki Electronics Industries Ltd.

Manufacturer

Matshushi Kotobuki Electronics Industries Ltd.

Photographer

Matshushi Kotobuki Electronics Industries Ltd.

Product

Eye Phone

Complete virtual reality system.

Designers

Doug Satzger, Nick Top—

IDEO Product Development;

Ann Laskoharuill—V.P.L.

Manufacturer

V.P.L.

Photographer

Rick English

Product

Frox Home Theater

System

Complete audio/video

system with state-of-the-art

digital sound.

Designer

Mark Biasotti

Manufacturer

Frox Inc.

Photographer

Rick English

Product

Concept for a Table Phone

Phone concept with clean

lines and compact design.

Designers

Michel Arney, principal

industrial designer;

David Harting, principal

mechanical engineer—

Design Continuum Inc.

Manufacturer

Advanced American

Electronics, Cambridge, MA

Photographer

Design Continuum Inc.

Product

ISDN Videophone

Interchangeable facade con-

tains color LCD, camera,

speaker, microphone, codec.

Designers

Produk Entwicklung Roericht

Melzer ID Konstanz

Manufacturer

Dornier Deutsche Aerospace,

Friedrichshafen, Germany

Photographer

Horst Eifert, Ulm

Product

IT-A3000

Telephone/digital answering

machine allows user to skip, or

repeat messages.

Designer

Sony Design Center

Manufacturer

Sony Corporation

Photographer

Sony Corporation

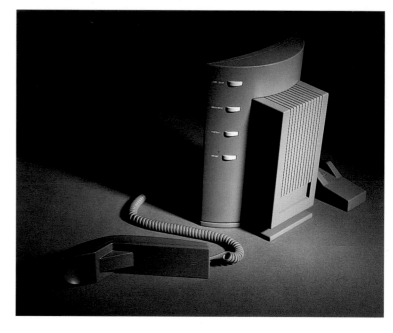

Product

Videophone

Residential 2-way video

phone with panoramic

curved surface.

Designers

Dan Harden, Tino Melzer—

frogdesign inc.

Manufacturer

Compression Labs, Inc.

Photographer

Steve Moeder

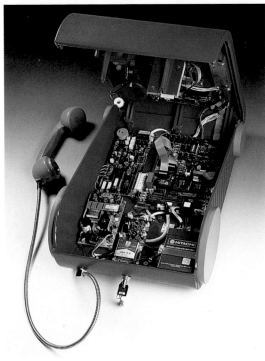

Product

T.M.S. Telephone

Multi-purpose telephone with

electronic payment.

Designer

Novodesign

Manufacturer

Sibs

Photographer

Novodesign

Product

**Business Telephone
Systems Series**
Simple, expandable systems
with planar designs.
Designers
Karim Rashid
Axis Group
Ian Norton
Manufacturer
VIDAR - Sun Moon Star,
Tai Pen
Photographer
Axis Group

Product

**FuturePhone: Executive
Information Center**
Relies on voice processing and
magnetic media to input data.
Designers
Dictaphone Industrial Group
Cousins Design
Manufacturer
Concept
Photographer
John Stuart

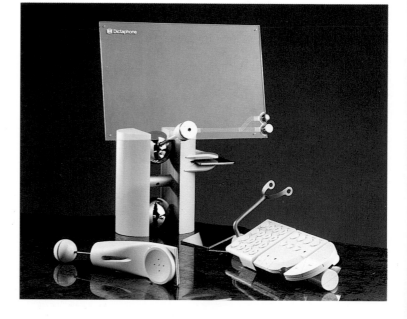

Product

**PROSET Professional Telephone
Headset**

Supported on a single ear by
hanger; speaker rests against the ear.

Designers

**Christopher Leow, industrial design;
Lawrence Schubert, Chris Lada,
mechanical engineering—
IDEO Product Development**

Manufacturer

UNEX

Photographer

Stan Musilek

Product

HelloShot Solo

On-the-ear headset; replace-
able ear cushions, removable
speaker for right/left ear use.

Designers

**Jim Sacherman,
Tom Shoda,
Malcolm Smith—
Palo Alto Design Group, Inc.**

Manufacturer

Hello Direct

Photographer

**Ric Deliantoni, C & I
Photography**

Product

Alcatel 8610 Telecom

System

Call simulator for telephone

exchanges.

Designer

J. Peter Klein,

Design Form Technik AG

Manufacturer

Alcatel STR AG

Photographer

Alexander Bayer

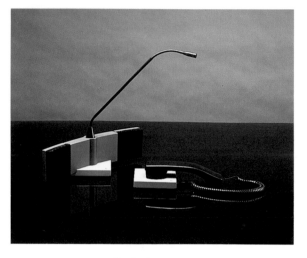

Product

Emergency Dispatch System

Organizes components into

functional modular design.

Designers

Gianfranco Zaccai, director of

design; Christopher Choido, senior

industrial designer; Luis Pedraza,

principal industrial designer;

David Harting, principal mechani-

cal engineer—

Design Continuum Inc.

Manufacturer

Advanced American Electronics,

Cambridge, MA

Photographer

Design Continuum Inc.

Product

3495 Tape Library

Dataserver

Manages and automates
retrieval, mount/demount
and storage of cartridges.

Designer

Martin J. Marotti

Manufacturer

IBM

Photographer

Jeffrey Muir Hamilton

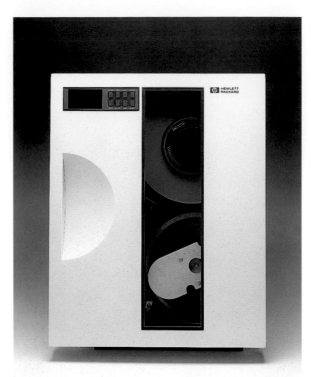

Product
HP88781A Tape Drive
Vertically oriented tape drive
for data storage/ retrieval.
Designers
Mo Khovaylo
Jim Dow
Manufacturer
Hewlett-Packard Company
Photographer
Jonathan Mankin

Product

Molecular Dynamics

FluorImager 575

Scans and analyzes molecular
sample using new fluorescent
technology.

Designers

Matt Barthelemy, project

manager, industrial design-

er; Ken Wood, industrial

design; Jeff Smith, design

principal

Manufacturer

Molecular Dynamics

Photographer

Rick English

Product

ITT Night Mariner

Amplifies available light up to
2000 times, allowing boaters
to see at night.

Designers

Mark Gildersleeve,

Dennis Huguley,

Jamey Boiter,

Bob Gibson,

Edgar Montague—

Machen Montague, Inc.

Manufacturer

ITT

Photographer

Steve Knight

Product

P.A.T. System (Personal

Athletic Trainer)

Monitors and records
work-out session.

Designers

Edward Boyd,

Tracy Teague,

Jim Naderi—

Machen Montague, Inc.

Manufacturer

Isotechnologies, Inc.

Photographer

David Ramsey

Product

Spectrum Analyzer

Hand-held diagnostic tool
identifies defects in large
industrial machinery.

Designers

Mark Stella,

Kuni Masuda,

Sohrab Vossoughi—

ZIBA Design Team

Manufacturer

Ono Sokki Corp. Ltd.

Photographer

Michael Jones

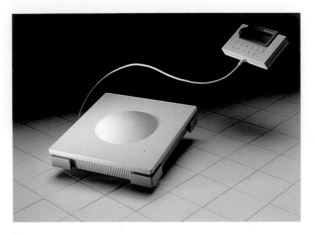

Product

Smart Scale

Records weight data and sum-
marizes information in bar
graph over week/month/year.

Designers

Tom Froning,

Sohrab Vossoughi—

ZIBA Design Team

Manufacturer

Tanita Corporation

Photographer

Michael Jones

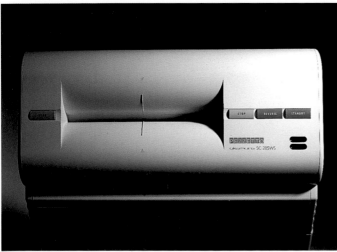

Product

**"Pezzetto" Office Paper
Shredder**

Paper shredder with newly
developed cutter and small
footprint for minimal noise.

Designers

**Hiroshi Mitsui, Udo Schill—
open house inc.**

Manufacturer

Okamura Corp.

Photographer

Kenj Wakairo

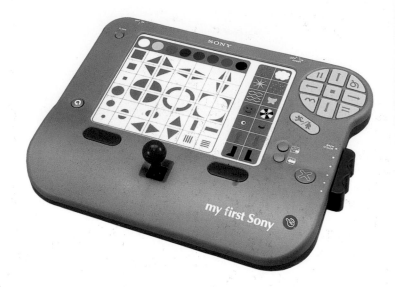

Product

HB-A5700 My First Sony®

Electronic Sketchpad

Allows child to draw color pic-

tures that appear on a TV

screen.

Designer

Sony Design Center

Manufacturer

Sony Corporation

Photographer

Sony Corporation

Product

HB-B7070 My First Sony®

Animation Computer

Draws color pictures,

animation on TV screen.

Designer

Sony Design Center

Manufacturer

Sony Corporation

Photographer

Sony Corporation

Product

Talk Dirty Translator

Six language translator

for swear words.

Designer

Chris Lenart, frogdesign inc.

Manufacturer

Hexaglot

Photographer

Steve Moeder

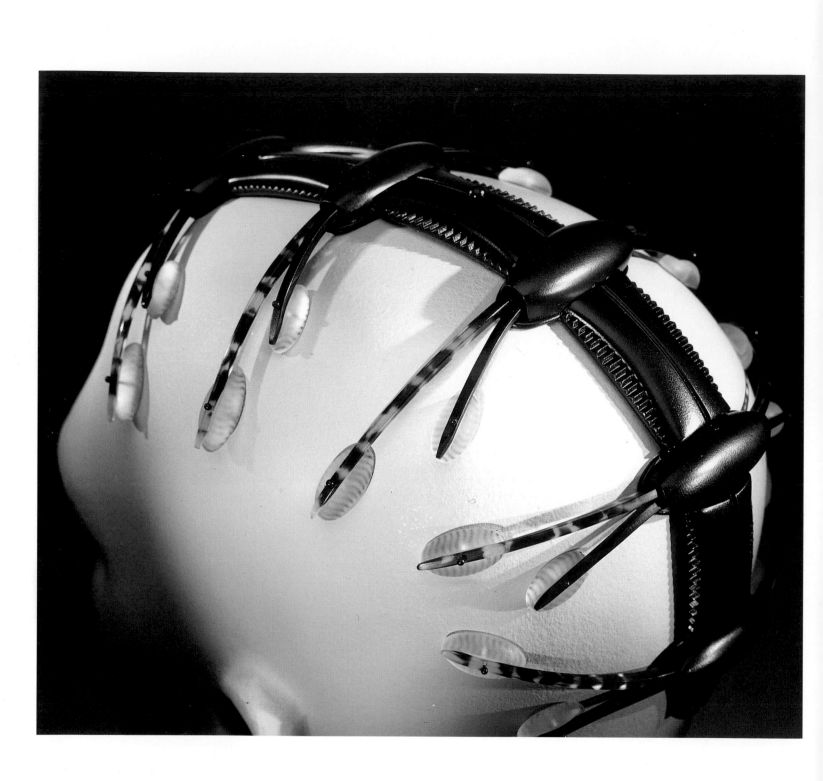

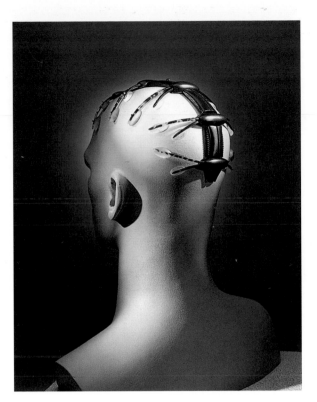

Product

The Passive

Communicator

Allows exchange of thoughts

and experiences presently

communicated through

sight and sound.

Designer

Donald Carr

Manufacturer

Concept **funded by**

NCR Corporation

Photographer

Tom Wedell

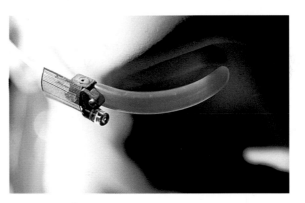

Product

Nirvware Cyberdesk

Pliable garment extends user's
senses; communicates with
full-color video linkage.

Designer

Krohn Design

Photographer

Lisa Krohn

Think of our human artifacts as prosthetic devices. Think about a spear as an extension of your arms, shoes as extensions of your feet, and a pencil as an extension of your mind. Pretty quickly, you'll be looking at everything from blenders to lawn mowers in a very different way.

When appliances are seen as extensions of our bodies, criteria for function and usability are much more obvious, much more sensible, and even much more fun. Man-made barriers will seem nonsensical and "universal design" will be a quaint relic.

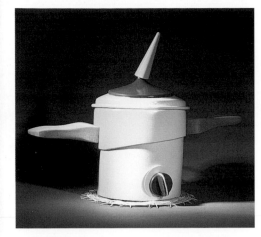

Product

"Wizard of Oz" Appliances

Series of domestic appliances
inspired by the cinematic
classic *The Wizard of Oz*:

Oz dishwasher

Scarecrow crock pot

Dorothy toaster

Tin Man coffee maker

Wicked Witch blender

Lion electric tea kettle

Glinda ice cream maker

Designer

Laurence Leon

Manufacturer

Prototypes

Photographer

Keith Piacensy

Product

Aroma Brew™

Designed to compete with
styling of Braun, yet sell at
price of Proctor-Silex.

Designers

Agostinho Martins

James Stewart

Chris Gieda

James Howard

Manufacturer

Melitta, USA

Photographer

Joseph Meacham

Product

Coffee Maker

Features rounded form and
transparent shower dome for
visible extraction of coffee.

Designer

Takashi-Sato

Manufacturer

**Matsushita Electric
Industrial Co., Ltd.**

Photographer

**Matsushita Electric
Industrial Co., Ltd.**

Product
FilterFresh
Coffee vending/dispensing
machine; brews each cup
or carafe individually.
Designers
**Tom Froning,
Song Kee Hong,
Sohrab Vossoughi—
ZIBA Design Team**
Manufacturer
VKI Corporation
Photographer
Michael Jones

Product
Coffee Maker
Ten-cup coffee maker.
Designer
frogdesign inc.
Manufacturer
Melitta
Photographer
Dietmar Henneka

Product
**"Rocopot"
Water-purifying Pot**
Charcoal filter purifies water.
Designers
**Fumikazu Masuda
Hideya Kurosaki—
open house inc.**
Manufacturer
Kuritac Corp.
Photographer
Kuniaki Okada

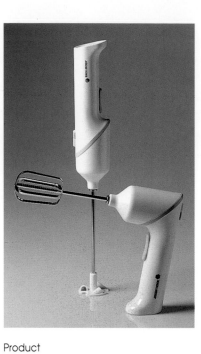

Product

Primo Toaster

Toaster for petit dejeuner.

Designer

Frechin et Bureaux

Manufacturer

SEB sa

Photographer

Mafalda Minette

Product

Cordless Handy Mixer

Switches from mixer to blender

with twist of wrist.

Designers

Gary Van Deursen

Greg Hoffmann

Manufacturer

Black & Decker

Photographer

Peter Orkin

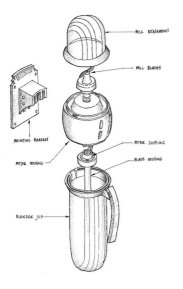

MILL ATTACHMENT

MILL BLADES

MOUNTING BRACKET

MOTOR COUPLING

MOTOR HOUSING

BLADE HOUSING

BLENDER JUG

Product

"Fusion" Kitchen Blender

Wall-mounted blender with

coffee mill attachment.

Designer

Stuart Harvey Lee

Manufacturer

Concept

Photographer

Stuart Harvey Lee

Product

Mediterraneo

Water tap combines classic

form with modern design.

Designer

Paolo Pedrizzetti

Manufacturer

F.LLI Fantini s.p.a.

Photographer

Giorgio Gugnani

Product

Dalomix

Water faucet with sensor-

based technology.

Designer

frogdesign inc.

Manufacturer

DAL

Photographer

frogdesign inc.

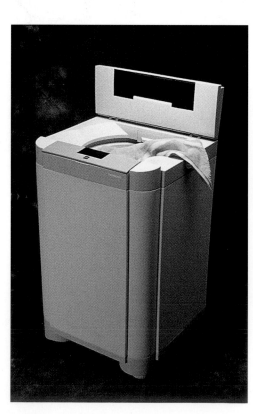

Product

Washing Machine

Space efficient with

minimal controls.

Designers

Michel Arney,

John Costello, principal

industrial designers—

Design Continuum Inc.

Manufacturer

Samsung Electronics,

America, Saddle Brook, NJ

Photographer

Design Continuum Inc.

Product

**The Metaform™ Personal
Hygiene System**

A universal design
concept for a bathroom
appropriate for all ages
and abilities.

Designers

**Gianfranco Zaccai,
director of design;
Luis Pedraza, Noelle Dye,
principal industrial designers;
Tim Dearborn, senior
industrial designer; Arthur
Rousmaniere, Andrew Ziegler,
Rich Miller, principal mechanical engineers; Jim Stark,
senior mechanical engineer—
Design Continuum Inc.**

Manufacturer

**Herman Miller Inc.
Zeeland, MI**

Photographer

Design Continuum Inc.

Product

Éman

Toothbrush with magnetic

support system.

Designer

Pascal Grossiord

Manufacturer

Prototype

Photographer

Pierre Anthoine

Product

Ultrasonic Toothbrush

Easily held, used; more

comfort and control.

Designers

John Costello, principal

industrial designer;

Ben Beck, senior

industrial designer—

Design Continuum Inc.

Manufacturer

Sonex International Inc.

Brewster, NY

Photographer

Design Continuum Inc.

Product

Electric Shaver "Catch"

Compact shaver with

built-in charger.

Designer

Fumikazu Masuda,

Indecs Inc.

Manufacturer

Mitsubishi Electric Corp.

Photographer

Junichi Kaizuka

Product

Sensor For'Women

Reusable razor addresses

needs of female shaving.

Designer

Jill Shurtleff

Manufacturer

The Gillette Company

Photographer

Michael Pruzan

Product

Electric Fan F-C309J

Four-speed fan. Thermosensor for

automatic operation,

wireless remote.

Designer

Hiroshi Miyake,

Matsushita Seiko Co., Ltd.

Manufacturer

Hiroshi Miyake,

Matsushita Seiko Co., Ltd.

Photographer

Hiroshi Miyake,

Matsushita Seiko Co., Ltd.

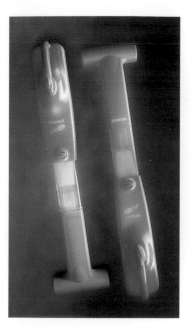

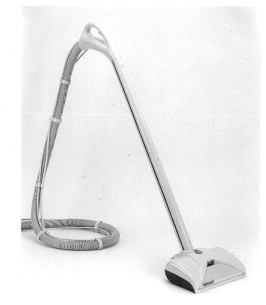

Product

BISSELL Trio

Convenience product does
numerous, frequent "all
around" cleaning tasks.

Designers

Bissell Industrial

Design, Grand Rapids, MI

INNO, Atlanta, GA

Manufacturer

Bissell, Inc.

Photographer

Craig Vander Lende

Product

BISSELL Power Brush

Carpet cleaning machine
with 40% fewer parts.

Designer

Brenda Reath,

Bissell Industrial Design

Manufacturer

Bissell, Inc.

Photographer

Phil Schaafsma

Product

Mulchinator® Cordless

Mulching Mower

Ninety minutes of mowing
time on single charge.

Designers

Alex Chunn,

Adrian Hartz,

Keith Long—

Ryobi Motor Products Corp.

Jim Watson,

Doug Alsup—

Alsup Watson Associates

Manufacturer

Ryobi Motor Product Corp.

Photographer

Bjorn Schulze

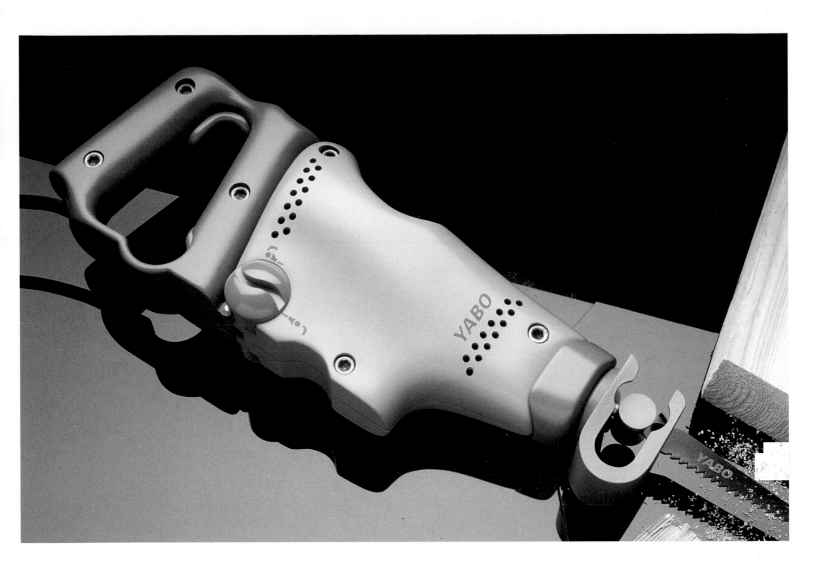

Product

Gig-Saw

Serves as jig saw or

reciprocating saw.

Designer

Frank Sterpka

Manufacturer

Concept

Photographer

Rick Whittey

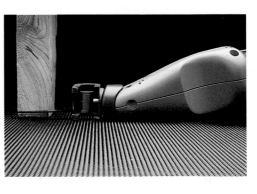

Product
Océa
Pocket knife with
transparent handle.
Designer
Pascal Grossiord
Manufacturer
Prototype
Photographer
Pascal Grossiord

Product

Odéo

Plastic watering can with
extensive tube, water level
indicator, and nozzle.

Designer

Pascal Grossiord

Manufacturer

Prototype

Photographer

Denis Rigault

Product

Cellaria

Polypropylene chopping board,
stainless steel knife.

Designer

Kazuo Kawaski

Manufacturer

Takefu Knife Village Assoc.

Photographer

Fujitsaka Mitsamasa

Product

**ClearVision II Handheld
Magnifiers**

Magnifiers with specially
designed handles.

Designers

Gordon Randall Perry

Richard Fienbloom

Manufacturer

Designs For Vision, Inc.

Photographer

Bill Waltzer

Product

BINI

Combination bookend and
floppy disk stand.

Designer

Kazuo Kawaski

Manufacturer

SIG Workshop Co., Ltd.

Photographer

Fujitsaka Mitsamasa

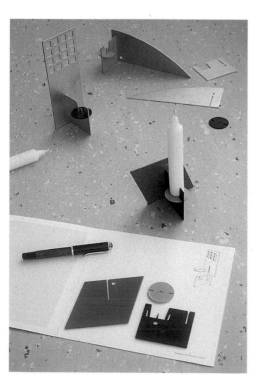

Product

Art Candle Kit

Portable flat candle kit can be
used as stationery.

Designer

Winfried Scheuer

Manufacturer

Emform, Germany

Photographer

Winfried Scheuer

Product

Ark of Noah

Environmentally friendly con-

ceptual writing device uses

branch and sand.

Designer

Vincent Shum Yiu Man

Manufacturer

Az Gallery, Tokyo, Japan

Photographer

Vincent Shum Yiu Man

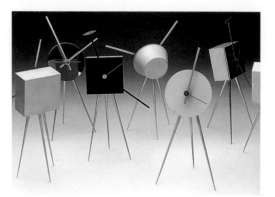

Products

Abaxial 1 and Abaxial 2

Mantle clocks made of cast
and conical spun aluminum.

Designer

Karim Rashid

Manufacturer

Gallery 91, New York, NY

Photographers

Tod Babick

Lesley Horowitz

Product

Mikros Hola

Table clock made of ABS,
available in 9 colors.

Designer

Kazuo Kawaski

Manufacturer

Takata Lemnos Inc.

Photographer

Fujitsaka Mitsamasa

Product

Wall Thermostat

Wall-mounted thermostat for

commercial/residential use.

Designers

Chris Alviar,

Sohrab Vossoughi—

ZIBA Design Team

Manufacturer

Cadet Manufacturing, Inc.

Photographer

ZIBA Design

E ver since I visited Alvar Aalto's Paimio sanatorium in Finland, I have looked at medical equipment from a completely different perspective. I always knew that design was tremendously powerful, but Aalto proved that design has the power to heal.

All too often, designers approach medical equipment with the same mindset that they bring to the design of sports equipment or office furniture. They think a lot about ergonomics but they could spend more time thinking about mortality, the fragile nature of human life and how form, color, and context can nurture life.

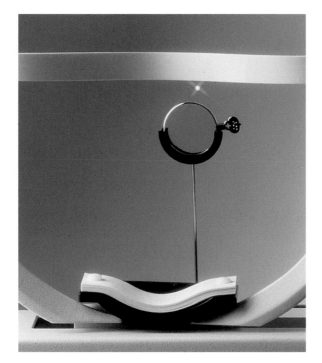

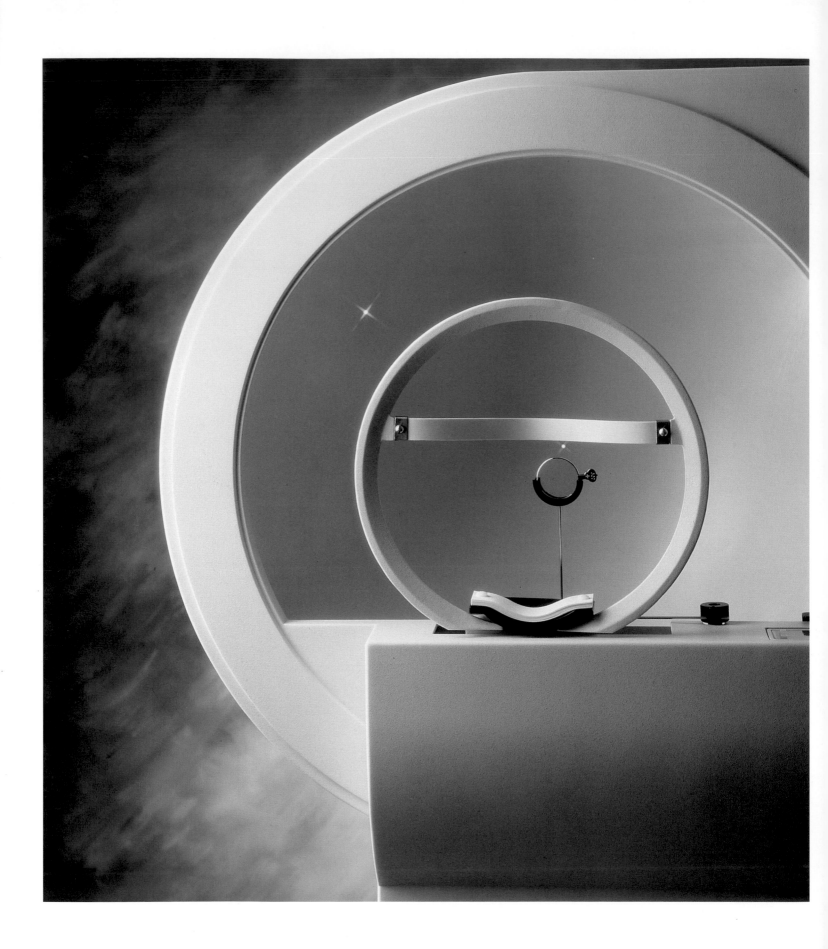

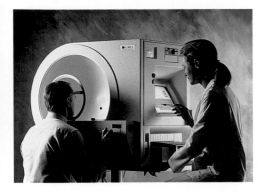

Product

Tomey 670 Perimeter

Used for visual field analysis in
diagnosis and treatment of
glaucoma patients.

Designer

Bryan Hotaling,

Product Insight, Inc.,

Acton, MA

Manufacturer

Tomey Technology, Inc.

Photographer

Steve Robb, Boston, MA

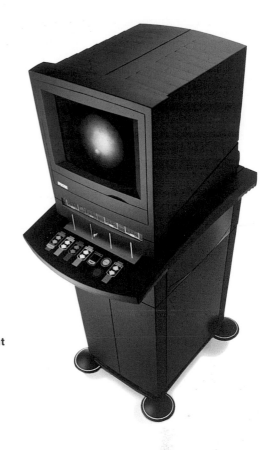

Product

Microprobe Ophthalmic

Laser Endoscope

Integrates laser technology
with microendoscopy.

Designers

Roberto Fraquelli,

John Stoddard—

IDEO Product Development

Manufacturer

ENDO OPTICS, USA

Photographer

IDEO

Product

LA350

Lens analyzer guides specialists
through analysis of glass/con-
tact lenses, or lens blanks.

Designers

Frank Friedman,

Steve Wittenbrock,

senior designers;

Glenn Polinsky, designer—

Soma, Inc.

Manufacturer

Humphrey Instruments Inc.

Photographer

Damian Conrad

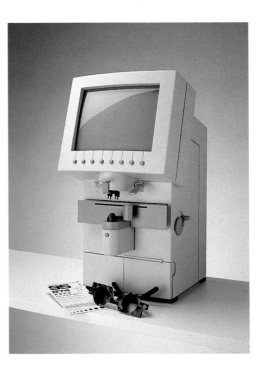

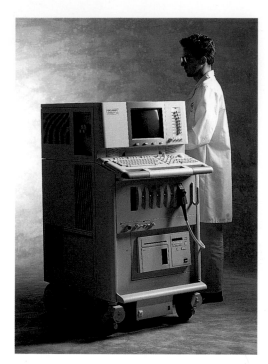

Product

**Medical Ultrasound Imaging
System**

Enhanced user interface,
convenient probe storage, and
footrest for managing cables.

Designers

**Naoto Fukasawa, Tim Parsey,
industrial design—
IDEO Product Development**

Manufacturer

Acuson Corporation

Photographer

Stan Musilek

Product

Excimer Laser (LAISer II)

Used for interventional cardiology;
promotes mobility, accessibility
for service.

Designers

**John von Buelow,
Ernesto Quinteros,
David Stocks,
Karell Slovacek—
S.G. Hauser Associates, Inc.**

Manufacturer

**LAIS (Advanced
Intervention Systems)**

Photographer

Terry Sutherland

Product

Drake Willock System 1000

Dialysis Machine

Purifies blood of patients

with kidney disease.

Designers

Paul Furner, Henry Chin,

Tom Froning, Dave Knaub,

Terry Jones, Sohrab

Vossoughi—

ZIBA Design Team

Manufacturer

Altin CD Medical, Inc.

Photographer

ZIBA Design

Product

Ventricular (Heart) Assist

System

Portable system supports

diseased or damaged hearts

waiting for transplant.

Designers

Naoto Fukasawa, Robin Sarre,

industrial design,

Tim Parsey, project manage-

ment, industrial design,

Jane Fulton, human factors—

IDEO Product Development

Manufacturer

Baxter Heatlhcare Corporation,

Novacor Division

Photographer

Charles Kemper

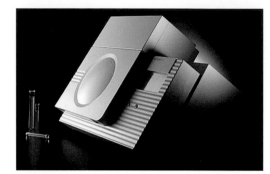

Product

Horizon Infusion Pump

Allows two pumps to be mounted
on IV poles in vertical space previously
used by one.

Designers

Tim Parsey, industrial design,

Peter Spreenberg, interaction design,

Jane Fulton, human factors,

Tony Fields, Walt Conti,

mechanical engineering—

IDEO Product Development

Manufacturer

McGaw, Inc.

Photographer

Giampiero Benvenuti

Product

Eclipse Blood Analyzer

Provides faster, more convenient blood test results.

Designers

Chris Alviar,

Terry Jones,

Sohrab Vossoughi—

ZIBA Design Team

Manufacturer

Biotope Corporation

Photographer

ZIBA Design

Product

Irma Blood Gas System

Immediate Response Mobile
Analysis (IRMA) provides on-
site blood gas analysis.

Designers

Eric Mueller

Tighe Belden

Danny Cunigan

Jeff Madison

Manufacturer

Diametrics Medical, Inc.

Photographer

Stan Waldhauser

Product

Impralert

Surgical/dental safety

system detects punctures

in surgical gloves.

Designers

Tom Froning,

Sohrab Vossoughi—

ZIBA Design Team

Manufacturer

IMPRA Corporation

Photographer

Michael Jones

Product

Biojector 2000

Non-invasive, self-contained
injection system delivers
medication without needle.

Designers

Rob Dillon,

Sohrab Vossoughi—

ZIBA Design team

Manufacturer

Bioject Inc.

Photographer

Michael Jones

Product

Angioplasty Indeflator

Surgical device to
facilitate circulation.

Designers

Nelson AU, industrial design,

vae Sun, engineering—

IDEO Product Development;

Chris Tacklund

Manufacturer

Advanced Cardiovascular

Systems (ACS)

Photographer

Geoffrey Nelson

Product

APL™ Automatic Pressure
Limiting Valve

Disposable pressure relief
valve regulates oxygen flow
to infant's lungs after birth.

Designers

Ralph DeVito

Tom Uhl

James Howard

Manufacturer

Vital Signs, Inc.

Photographer

Tom Del Guercio

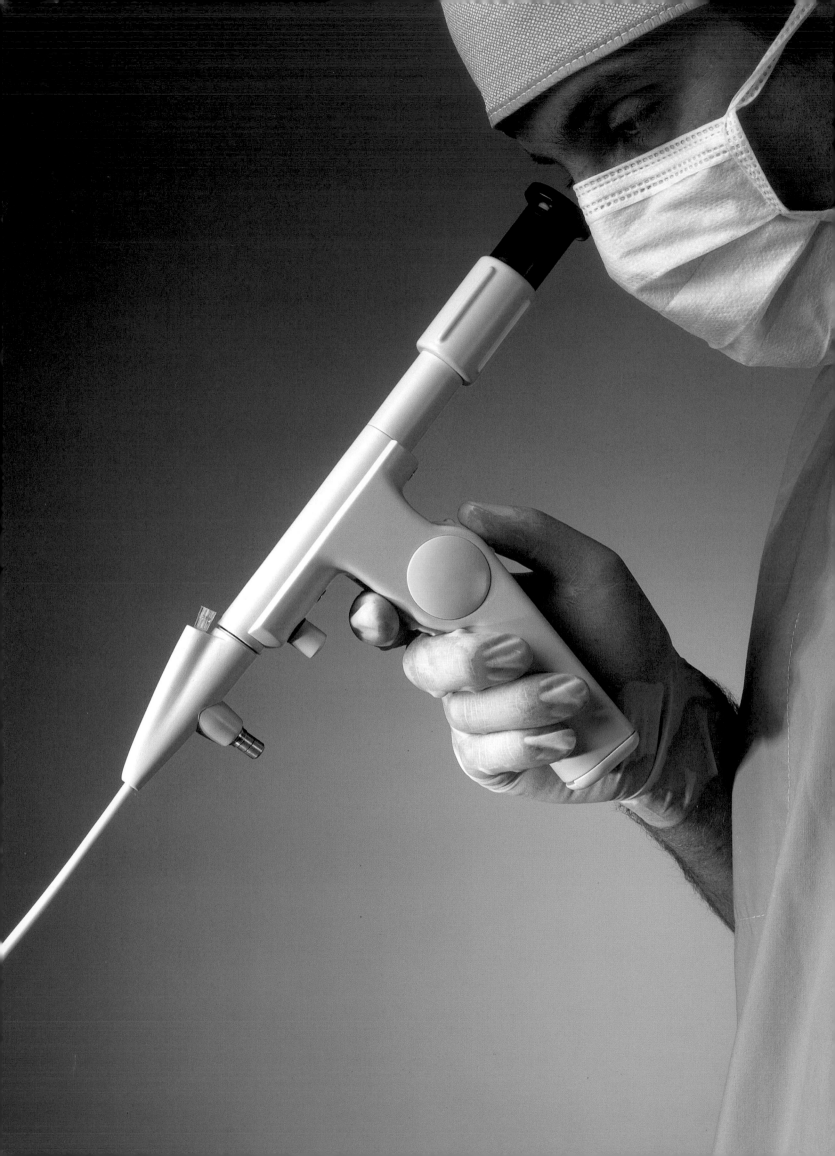

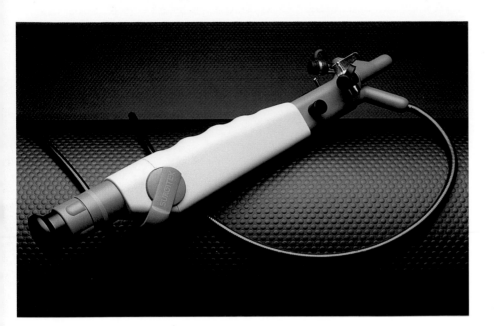

Product

Schott/Surgitek Flexible Endoscope

Specially placed and angled thumb lever reduces fatigue.

Designer

Robert Bruno, Group Four Design

Manufacturer

Schott/Surgitek

Photographer

Rick Whittey

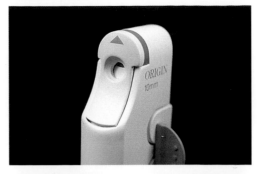

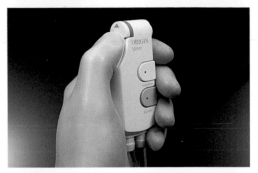

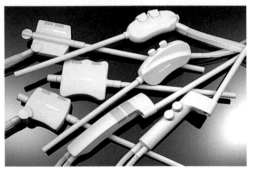

Product

Endoscope

Single-hand operation allows surgeon to direct light source within patient.

Designers

Steven Montgomery,

Mark Anderson,

Paul Gaudio,

David Stocks—

S.G. Hauser Associates, Inc.

Photographer

Terry Sutherland

Product

Laproscopic Suction/Irrigation Device

Allows second laproscopic instrument to be inserted through back of unit.

Designers

Mark Steiner, Steiner Design Associates;

Jeff Stein, John Harrison, synthetic engineering

Manufacturer

MEDTECH Group for Origin Medsystems, Inc.

Photographer

Mark Steiner

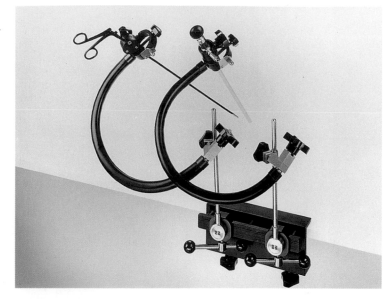

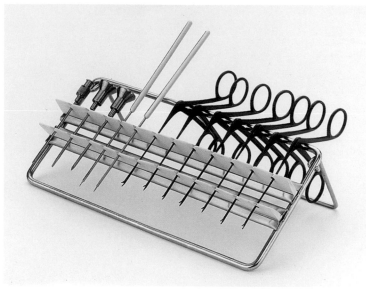

Product

Surgissistant™

Universally flexible arm

system fastens instruments

to operating table.

Designers

Linda Celentano

Herbert Schainholz

Manufacturer

Medin Corporation

Photographer

John Parsekian

Product

Medical Instrumentation

Sterilization Racks

Surgical steel racks secured

into silicone rubber cradles.

Designers

Linda Celentano

Pat Jaramillo

Jay Schainholz

Manufacturer

Medin Corporation

Photographer

John Parsekian

Product

Medical Sterilization Trays

for Instrumentation

Perforated metal trays

organize instrumentation

for sterilization.

Designers

Pat Jaramillo

Herbert Schainholz

Linda Celentano

Manufacturer

Medin Corporation

Photographer

John Parsekian

Product

BioTrac

Simple organizing tool

for lab technicians.

Designers

Mark Stella,

Sohrab Vossoughi—

ZIBA Design Team

Manufacturer

Biotope Corporation

Photographer

ZIBA Design

Product

labIntelligence HPGE 1000
DNA Analyzer
Automates DNA analysis; fan
and heat dispersion system,
indented window for viewing.
Designers
Jeff Smith, design principal;
Max Yoshimoto, project
manager, industrial design;
Gerard Furbershaw, Bjarki
Hallgrimsson, product design
Manufacturer
labIntelligence
Photographer
Rick English

Product

Park Scientific AutoProbe
Scanning Tunneling
Microscope
Computer-driven microscope
for imaging nanometer scale
features on samples.
Designers
Gerard Furbershaw, design
principal; Max Yoshimoto,
project manager, industrial
design; Gil Wong, industrial
design; Marieke van Wijnen,
Paul Hamerton-Kelly,
product design
Manufacturer
Park Scientific Instruments
Photographer
Rick English

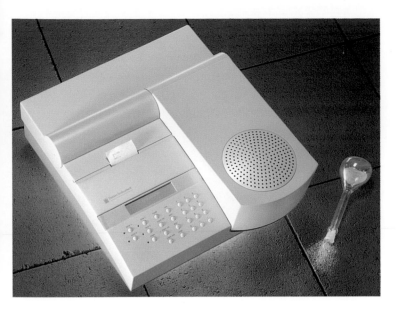

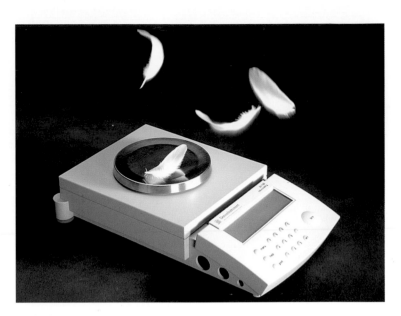

Product

Moisture Balance

Precision lab instrument

measures moisture content.

Designers

Chris Alviar,

Sohrab Vossoughi—

ZIBA Design Team

Manufacturer

Denver Instrument, Inc.

Photographer

ZIBA Design

Product

XD Scale

Used by scientists, researchers;

can be linked to printer or

network of instruments.

Designers

Chris Alviar,

Sohrab Vossoughi—

ZIBA Design Team

Manufacturer

Denver Instrument, Inc.

Photographer

Michael Jones

Product

Model DT93 Anatomy

Immersion Dissecting Table

Permits cadaver to be kept in

anatomy laboratory, residing

in solution filled tank.

Designers

John McBrayer,

McBrayer Industrial Design;

Bill Joiner,

KLN Steel Products

Manufacturer

KLN Steel Products,

San Antonio, TX

Photographer

Tracy Maurer

Product
Carna
Compact, foldable, light-
weight titanium wheelchair.
Designer
Kazuo Kawaski
Manufacturer
SIG Workshop Co., Ltd.
Photographer
Fujitsuka Mitsumasa

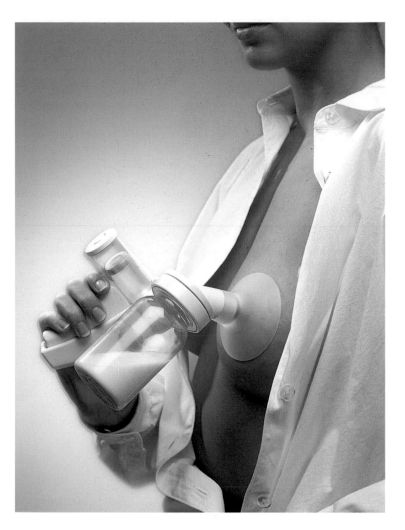

Product
Mia Breast Pump
Hand-held, manually
operated breast pump.
Designers
**Tom Shoda,
Dallas Grove—
Palo Alto Design Group**
Manufacturer
A-TCH Ltd.
Photographer
Rick English

Product
Monty Chair
Patient room chair for
healthcare facilities.
Designer
**Edgar Montague,
Machen Montague, Inc.**
Manufacturer
Images of America, Inc.
Photographer
David Hussey

For centuries, furniture design has been about the marriage, the separation, the reconciliation, and the relationship of the abstract concepts and physical realities of form and function. Tradition has leveled the playing field—a chair is a chair. As a result, furniture design tends to be a bit more philosophical.

Can an object simultaneously be personal and universal? Does form really equal function? What is form? What is function? What is a comfortable form? A comfortable function? A usable form? A usable function? Is it art or craft? What is a chair?

Furniture

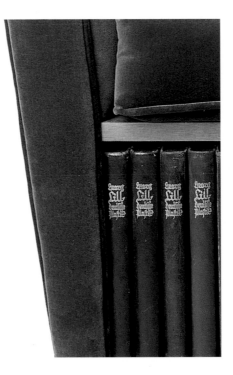

Product

Double or Nothing Series

Space-efficient, cost-
effective furniture series.

Designer

Marco Pasanella

Manufacturer

The Pasanella Company

Photographer

Kit Latham

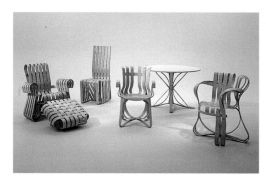

Product

The Gehry Collection

Lightweight, economical,

durable furniture made of

thin, laminated maple strips.

Designer

Frank Gehry

Manufacturer

The Knoll Group

Photographer

The Knoll Group

Product

"Otto"

Chair; back attaches to wall.

Designer

Stacy Walsh

Manufacturer

Prototype

Photographer

Stacy Walsh

Product

Juliet

Five drawer unit with

cloth covering.

Designer

Stacy Walsh

Manufacturer

Protoype

Photographer

Stacy Walsh

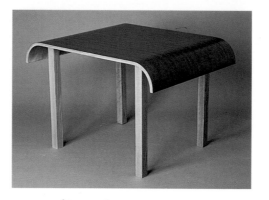

Product

Searstyle Furniture

Furniture collection inspired
by the cultural values of Sears.

Designer

Constantin Boym

Manufacturer

Prototypes

Photographer

Constantin Boym

Product

**Stainless/oxidized steel
furniture**

Structural as well as functional
furniture pieces; stainless
steel sheet, oxidized tubing.

Designer

Carl C. Martinez

Manufacturer

Carl C. Martinez

Photographer

Carl C. Martinez

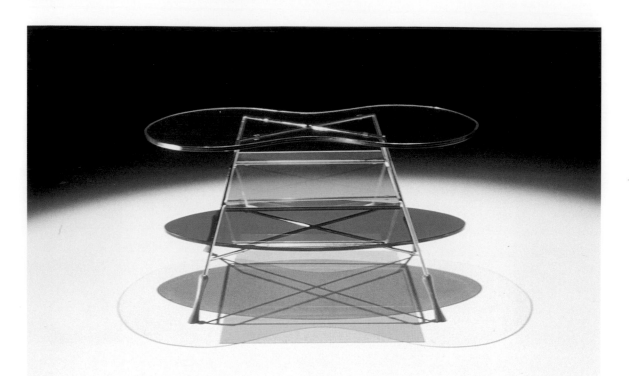

Product

Aura

Coffee table; colored glass
plates producible in 1600 hues
using Trecent technology.

Designer

**Karim Rashid, Karim
Rashid Industrial Design**

Manufacturers

**North Studio Inc., Toronto
Canada**

GFA, Los Angeles, CA

Photographer

Doug Hall

Product

Coffee Table

Glass top, steel base.

Designer

Fernd Van Engelen

Manufacturer

Section Five Design

Photographer

Fernd Van Engelen

Products

Lunar Design:

Conference Room Table

Lobby Coffee Table

Eye-catching centerpiece

for office entryway and

conference room.

Designers

Ken Wood

Dave Laituri

Manufacturer

Lunar Design

Photographer

Rick English

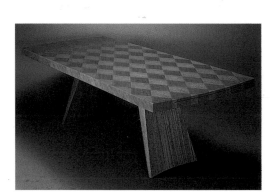

Product

Wonder Collection:

Wonder Table

Conference/dining table.

Polished anigre top in

diamond pattern.

Designer

Dakota Jackson

Manufacturer

Dakota Jackson Inc.

Photographer

Steve Tague

Product

"Andrews Sisters"

Set of three tables laminated

in bubinga wood.

Designer

Pedro Miralles

Manufacturer

Punt Mobles, S.L.

Photographer

Punt Mobles, S.L.

Product

Papallona

Console table with two

leaves of cherry.

Designers

Lola Castello

Vincent Martinez

Manufacturer

Punt Mobles, S.L.

Photographer

Punt Mobles, S.L.

Product

Liprai

Occasional table; top over-laid in silk-screened abet-print soft finish.

Designer

Sottsass Associati

Manufacturer

Zanotta Spa

Photographer

Marino Ramazzotti-Muggio

Product

Harrison Table

Table with interlocking patinated steel base folds flat for easy shipping/storage.

Designer

Clodagh

Manufacturers

Tony Conway *(base)*

New York Quarries *(top)*

Photographer

Daniel Aubry

Product

"Playback"

Wooden guest chair
with 10 back options.

Designer

Joe Ricchio,

Studio/Ricchio

Manufacturer

Atelier International

Photographer

Karant & Associates, Inc.

Product

Tribeca Chair

Intended for guest and side
chair applications in office.

Designers

Mark W. Goetz

Timothy H. Richartz

TZ Design

Manufacturer

Bernhardt Furniture

Company

Photographer

Omega Studios Inc.

Product

"Echo" Armchair

Birch plywood, cherry veneer.

Designer

David Mocarski

Manufacturer

Arkkit Forms Design

Photographer

Charles Imstepf

Product

Ke-'zu Open Arm Chair

Open grained ash arms and

legs; fully upholstered

seat and back.

Designer

Dakota Jackson

Manufacturer

Dakota Jackson Inc.

Photographer

Steve Tague

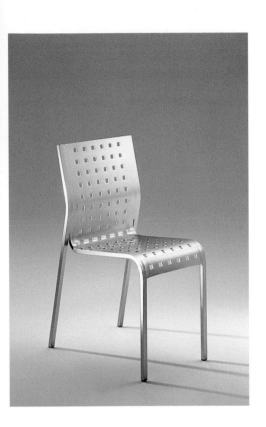

Product
Mirandolina
Stacking chair with/without
armrests.
Designer
Pietro Arosio
Manufacturer
Zanotta Spa
Photographer
Marino Ramazzotti-Muggio

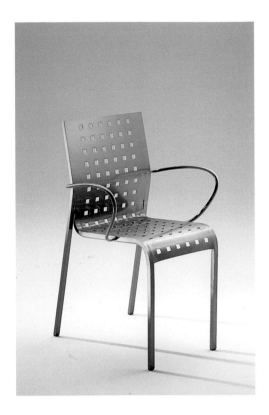

Product
Altera
Swivel armchair; removable
cover in oriente fabric, alcan-
tara, or leather.
Designer
Andrea Branzi
Manufacturer
Zanotta Spa
Photographer
Marino Ramazzotti-Muggio

Product

Wave Bench

Bench with understated
design can be used in bed-
room, front hall or terrace.

Designer

Clodagh

Manufacturers

Tony Conway (bench)

The Ashley Studios (upholstery)

Photographer

Daniel Aubry

Product

Disc Harrow Bench

Recalls memories of the
traditional farm.

Designer

Virginia Leigh Durfey

Manufacturer

Virginia Leigh Durfey

Photographer

James Beard

Product
Bistro' Table
Steel tube framework;
plate glass or black
laminated wood top.
Designer
Maurizio Peregalli
Manufacturer
Noto
Photographer
Noto

Product
Bistro' Barstool
Steel tube frame, alder heart
back, elm wood veneer; lami-
nated or padded seating.
Designer
Maurizio Peregalli
Manufacturer
Noto
Photographer
Noto

Product
Paulownia Bench and Chair
Designer
**Rei Kawakubo,
Comme des Garcons**
Manufacturer
Comme des Garcons
Photographer
Masayuki Hayashi

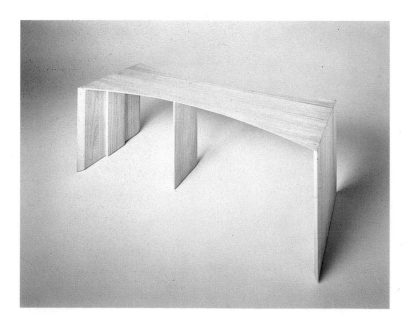

Product

ETA™ System Furniture

Furniture with interlocking
joinery assembles in minutes
without fasteners or tools.

Designer

Douglas M. Green

Manufacturer

Green Design Inc.

Photographer

Matt Spaulding

Product

"Dino" Table

Cafe table; bronzed sand
cast base, maple top.

Designer

Chris Collicott

Manufacturer

Chris Collicott

Photographer

Chris Collicott

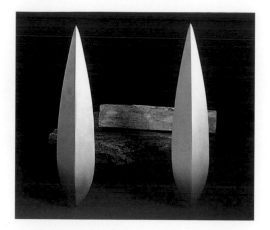

Product

Brass Andirons

Sand-casted solid brass; specially weighted base accommodates heavy logs.

Designers

Stephen Doyle

Miguel Oks

Manufacturer

Drenttel Doyle Projects

Photographer

Drenttel Doyle Projects

Product

Mosiac Furniture

Made of discarded furniture and stained glass scraps.

Designer

Chris Graziano

Manufacturer

Chris Graziano

Photographer

Chris Graziano

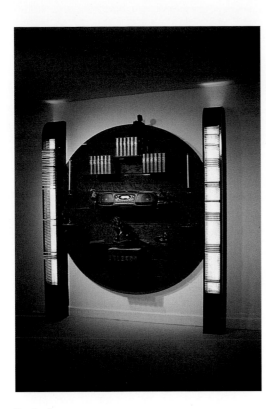

Product

Modular Library Rising Sun

CD storage unit with

fluorescent backlight.

Designer

Pascal Luthy

Manufacturer

Ebemistene Luthy SA

Photographer

Pascal Luthy

Product

Walk-up Bookcase

Horizontal stainless steel rungs

provide accessiblilty to higher

shelves without stool/ladder.

Designer

Clodagh

Manufacturer

Architectural Sculpture

Associates

Photographer

Daniel Aubry

Product

Living Systems: Grid Table

Modular components

are interchangeable

and versatile.

Designer

Harry Allen

Manufacturer

Harry Allen

Photographer

Liz Deschenes

Product

Le Lac Armchair

Wooden frame, bultex uphol-

stery covered in

fabric or leather.

Designer

Ecart Design

Manufacturer

Ecart International

Photographer

Deidi Von Schaewen

Product

Le Lac Sofa

Wooden frame, bultex foam

upholstery, covered in

fabric or leather.

Designer

Ecart Design

Manufacturer

Ecart International

Photographer

Deidi Von Schaewen

Product

Table de Verre

Nickel steel tube structure

with sandblasted glass top.

Designer

Ecart Design

Manufacturer

Ecart International

Photographer

Deidi Von Schaewen

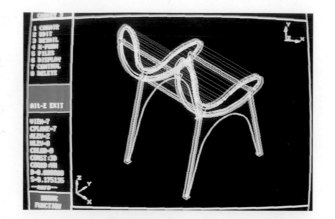

Product

ARP Chair Series

Stacking chairs; cantilevered
cherry plywood. ARP 2 has
elasticized webbing.

Designer

Karim Rashid

Manufacturer

**Area Group Inc., Toronto,
Canada**

Photographer

Doug Hall

Product

Decision

Sofa Series for reception areas

with combinable units.

Designer

Pelikan Design

Manufacturer

Fritz Hansens, Eft. A/S

Photographer

Pelikan Design

L ike moths, designers are attracted to light. And light is what makes lighting design challenging and dramatic. Lighting is often the jewelry of a room—the accent, the fashion accessory—but it's the object's output that creates and controls the moods and textures of the environment. So regardless of whether a designer is more focused on the hardware or the software of lighting, the magic comes in the combination.

This is a very inclusive category. Self-expression, craft, and experiments with new materials and technologies continually push lighting design to the limits and beyond.

Lighting

Product

Branch Lamps

Reconciles untamed spirit of
nature with rationality of
industrial materials.
Designer .

Krohn Design

Photographer

Lisa Krohn

Product

Lucellino

Table/wall light with hand-

finished, dove feather wings.

Designer

Ingo Maurer

Manufacturer

Ingo Maurer GmbH

Photographer

Tom Vack, Chicago, Milano

  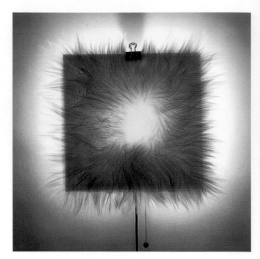

Products

Copy Light

Six of 27 lampshades

designed in different

countries for an exhibition.

Designers

Copy Light Concept:

Metamoderne,

Mathais Deitz, Deitz

Design Management

Shades from left to right:

Juli Capella, Quim Larrea

Filipe Alarcaó

Pedro Silva Dias

Siggi Fischer Woppertal

Aldo Cibic

Alberto Livore

Manufacturer

"Design Box"

Photographer

Bernd Hoff

  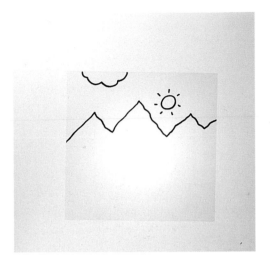

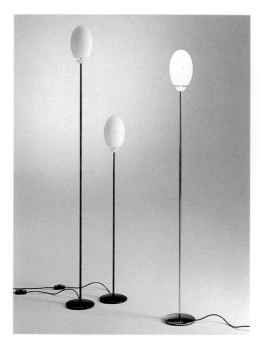  

Product

Brera

Hanging light; two diffusers provide continuous brightness.

Designer

Achille Castiglioni

Manufacturer

Flos Spa

Photographer

Flos Spa

Product

Musina

Table/floor lamp; diffusers in
translucent porcelain or
cobalt blue glass.

Designer

Maurizio Peregalli

Manufacturer

Noto

Photographer

Noto

Product

Aladino

Floor lamp with changable
shades in various designs.

Designer

Mathais Dietz, Frankfurt

Manufacturer

Belux, Wohlen

Photographer

Tom Vack

Product

Laurel

Steel stem, cast iron base,
aramid fiber paper diffuser.

Designer

Brent Markee

Manufacturer

Resolute

Photographer

Dan Langley

Product

Tijuca Wall

"Touch tronic" halogen wall-

mount with transformer-sensor-

dimmer.

Designers

Ingo Maurer and team

Manufacturer

Ingo Maurer GmbH

Photographer

Tom Vack, Chicago, Milano

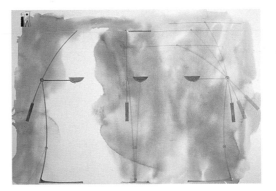

Product

"Yorick"

Halogen task lamp; counter-

balanced reflecting screen.

Designer

Beth Mosher

Manufacturer

Gallery 91

Photographers

Beth Mosher

Rick Loduha

Product

"Adam"

Halogen light with rubbery

groove for angle adjustment

of light source.

Designer

Vincent Shum Yiu Man

Manufacturer

BG Lighting, Hong Kong

Photographer

Vincent Shum Yiu Man

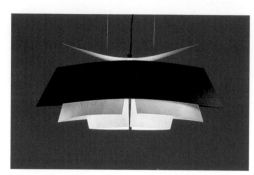

Product

Halcyon

Hand-painted in textured rust

finish sconce, available

with or without wings.

Designer

Michael Abrams

Manufacturer

Sirmos

Photographer

William Whitehurst

Product

Chapeau

Anodized aluminum body,

aramid paper diffuser.

Designer

Brent Markee

Manufacturer

Resolute

Photographer

Dan Langley

Product

Zig Zag Light

Joinable segments can be

mounted on the wall,

ceiling or suspended.

Designer

Clodagh

Manufacturers

Dan Chelsea

Tom Baer

Photographer

Daniel Aubry

Product

Jack

Wall/ceiling-mounted fixture

with full rotation/tilt.

Designers

Ingo Maurer

Franz Ringelhan

Manufacturer

Ingo Maurer GmbH

Photographer

Tom Vack, Chicago, Milano

Product

Light Lite

Lightweight, energy

efficient ceiling light.

Designer

Philippe Starck

Manufacturer

Flos Spa

Photographer

Flos Spa

Product

Lamp 0509

Desk lamp.

Designer

David Weeks

Photographer

David Weeks

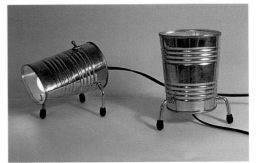

Product

Lamp 0508

Illuminates surfaces in

intimately lit areas.

Designer

David Weeks

Photographer

David Weeks

Product

Lamp 0501

Low cost decorative

table lamp.

Designer

David Weeks

Photographer

David Weeks

Product

Can Lamps

Family of three table lamps

and wall sconce.

Designers

Lisa Krohn

Martha Davis

Manufacturer

Gallery 91

Photographer

Lisa Krohn

Product

Beata Lamp

Patinated brass, metal mesh,

crystal; available with halogen

unit or candelabra socket.

Designer

Felipe Morales

Manufacturer

Flip Design

Photographer

Felipe Morales

Product

"Mira"

Incandescent table lamp;
chromed steel base, nylon diffuser over metal rings.

Designer

**Martha Davis, Gioia Gajo—
Able**

Manufacturer

Metal Mania

Photographer

Kenneth Willardt

Product

"Aura"

Incandescent table lamp;
chromed steel base, nylon
diffuser over metal rings.

Designer

Martha Davis, Able

Manufacturer

Metal Mania

Photographer

Kenneth Willardt

Product

Brioche Bistro Lamp

Maple stem, nickel base,
aramid fiber paper diffuser.

Designer

Brent Markee

Manufacturer

Resolute

Photographer

Dan Langley

Product

Prometheus Table Lamp

Molded glass panels, steel

base; fluorescent, halogen,

incandescent lamp options.

Designer

David Baird, Architect

Manufacturer

Ziggurat

Photographer

Alan Linn

Product

Motion 6

High-powered moisture-proof
pendant light for pools.

Designer

LD Yamagiwa Laboratory Ltd.

Manufacturer

Yamagiwa Corporation

Photographer

Misami Sato

Product

In•spiration No. 5

Wall lamp.

Designer

LD Yamagiwa Laboratory Ltd.

Manufacturer

Yamagiwa Corporation

Photographer

Misami Sato

Product

Edge Lit Exit Sign

Designers

**Will Goldschmidt, design
director; Chris Carmody,
designer; Irving Schaffer,
engineering director—
Designspring, Inc.**

Manufacturer

**AtLite Lighting
Equipment Inc.**

Photographer

Designspring, Inc.

Product

Walking Light

Compact, hand-free flashlight

with wide-angle movement,

and automatic on/off.

Designer

Satoru Usami

Manufacturer

Matsushita Battery

Industrial Co., Ltd.

Photographer

Matsushita Battery

Industrial Co., Ltd.

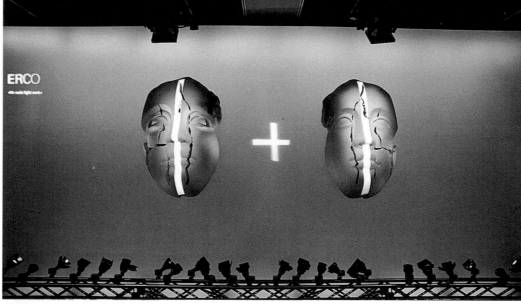

Products

**ERCO Spotlights and
Projectors at Hanover Fair**

Composition in lights featuring
ERCO products designed
by Uwe Belzner.

Designers

**ERCO Leuchten GmbH;
Uwe Belzner, lighting
designer**

Manufacturer

ERCO Leuchten GmbH

Photographer

ERCO Press

Product

Avalon Light Structure

Suspended direct,

indirect luminaire.

Designer

ERCO Leuchten GmbH

Manufacturer

ERCO Leuchten GmbH

Photographer

ERCO Press

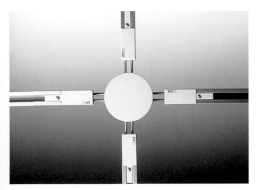

Product

Castor, Compar, Minirail

Designer

Alois Dworschak, ERCO

Manufacturer

ERCO Leuchten GmbH

Photographer

Axel Gnad

Product

Quinta

Spotlight allows rotation and

tilt angles to be independently

set and locked.

Designer

Knud Holscher

Manufacturer

ERCO Leuchten GmbH

Photographer

Axel Gnad

Textiles have long been on the cutting edge of design and technology. In fact, the ability to weave simple textiles helped propel *Homo sapiens* out of the Stone Age. Textiles were also the first industry in the Industrial Revolution. And today's powerful personal computers can trace their origins back to the Jacquard loom.

But the real contribution of textiles has been to the development of human culture. No other medium, not television or even books, has had the continuing impact on culture that textiles have had.

Textiles

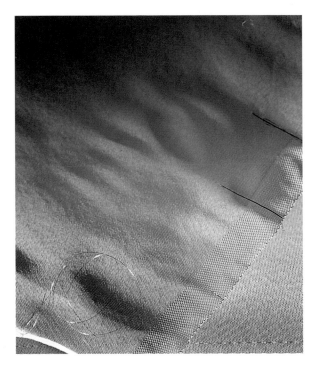

Product

Colored Metal Cloth

Nylon/polyester blend created with plain weave and
hand dying technique.

Designer

Reiko Sudo

Manufacturer

NUNO Corporation

Photographer

Sue McNab

Product

Copper Cloth

Made with two kinds of
thread; promix in the warp
and copper wire in the weft.

Designer

Reiko Sudo

Manufacturer

NUNO Corporation

Photographer

Sue McNab

Product

Cracked Cloth Newspaper

Polyester with newspaper
print created by print and
welding technique.

Designer

Reiko Sudo

Manufacturer

NUNO Corporation

Photographer

Sue McNab

Product

Checked Tabby

Made of transparent nylon
yarn with cotton warps and
twisted cotton wefts.

Designer

Reiko Sudo

Manufacturer

NUNO Corporation

Photographer

Sue McNab

Product

Cracked Cloth

Polyester organdy bonded
with rayon cloth that is burned
out to create pattern.

Designer

Reiko Sudo

Manufacturer

NUNO Corporation

Photographer

Sue McNab

Product

"Floramania"

Hand knotted area rug; large
scale forms and traditional
Indian paisley textile motifs.

Designer

Christine Van Der Hurd

Manufacturer

Christine Van Der Hurd, Inc.

Photographer

Rob Gray

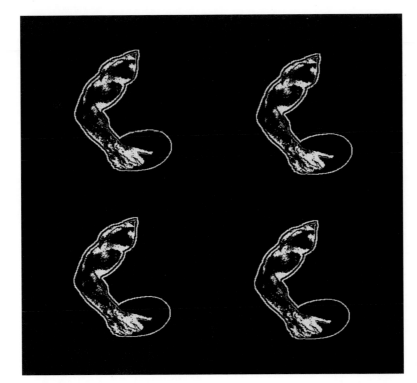

Product

Arm 1

Cotton/acrylic face to face

velvet upholstery.

Designer

Marc Van Hoe

Manufacturer

Erotex

Photographer

Marc Van Hoe

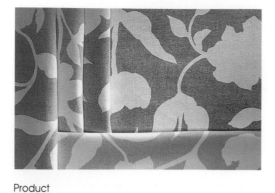

Product

Antique Garden

Linen/cotton print produced
with antiquing technique.

Designers

Lori Weitzner

Jack Lenor Larsen

Manufacturer

Jack Lenor Larsen

Photographer

Amos Chan

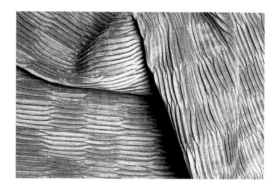

Product

Solace

Cotton/viscose voided velvet
with leaf pattern floating on a
satin ground.

Designers

Lori Weitzner

Jack Lenor Larsen

Manufacturer

Jack Lenor Larsen

Photographer

Amos Chan

Product

**Moonsoon, Tasket,
Accolade**

Metallic print, dot-square pattern, and plaid silks.

Designers

Lori Weitzner

Jack Lenor Larsen

Manufacturer

Jack Lenor Larsen

Photographer

Amos Chan

Product

Jacob's Ladder

Cotton/rayon velvet, pleated
to create 3-D look.

Designers

Lori Weitzner

Jack Lenor Larsen

Manufacturer

Jack Lenor Larsen

Photographer

Amos Chan

Product

Dragonseed

Cotton/silk blend with brilliant

coloring and gold flashes.

Designer

Larsen Design

Manufacturer

Jack Lenor Larsen

Photographer

Amos Chan

Product

Aqua Striped Scarf

Silk scarf made of 7 strips of
chiffon in iridescent
water tones.

Designer

Annie Walwyn-Jones

Manufacturer

**Annie Walwyn-Jones Ltd.,
New York, NY**

Photographer

Copyline Corp.

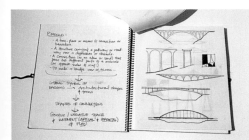

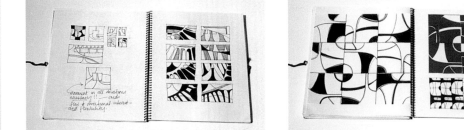

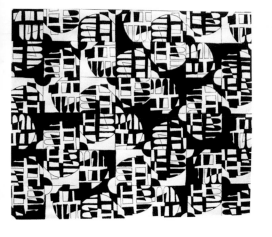

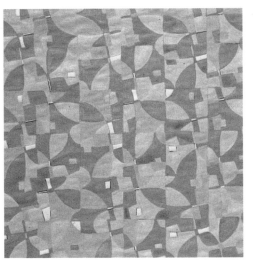

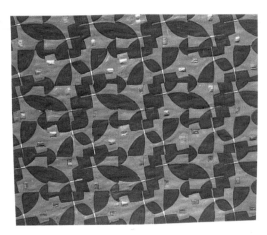

Product

"Bridging": Fabric/

Textiles for the Next Era

Textiles with intertwining

bridge patterns.

Designer

Shashi B. Caan

Manufacturer

Concept

Photographer

Shashi B. Caan

The design of tabletop objects may seem simple when compared with the complexity of electronic or medical equipment but the issues are equally sophisticated—they're just different.

Design opportunities are rare (and rarefied) when the typeforms are as distilled and the traditions are as established as they are in tabletop products. Tight parameters provoke designers' talents. The challenge of designing a better wine glass that is still a wine glass poses a classic set of design problems that are difficult, demanding, and ultimately very satisfying to solve.

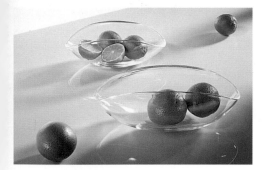

Products

"Folded Bowl"

"Medium Folded Bowl"

Glass bowls with simple

lines and curves.

Designer

Joel Smith

Manufacturer

Steuben, New York, NY

Photographer

Robert Moore Photography,

New York, NY

Product

Mobius Prism with

oak base

Pure crystal mobius prism.

Designer

Peter Drobny

Manufacturer

Steuben, New York, NY

Photographer

Robert Moore Photography,

New York, NY

Product

Tea Server

Sterling silver tea server.

Designer

Gordan Randall Perry

Manufacturer

Perry Design

Photographer

Gordon Randall Perry

Product

Lidded Vessel

Decorative metal vessel.

Designer

Michael Rowe

Manufacturer

Michael Rowe

Photographer

David Cripps

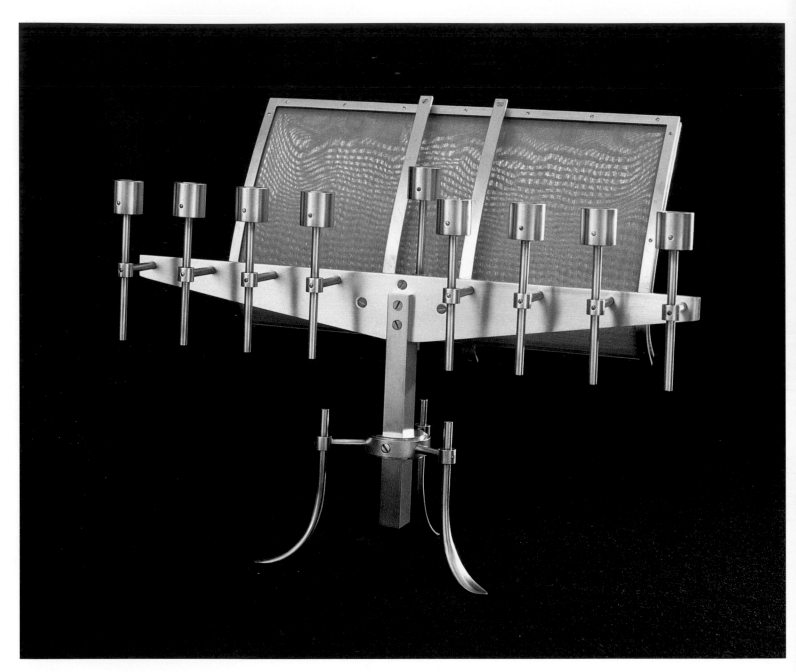

Product

Menorah

Matte nickel-plated brass,

stainless steel mesh.

Designer

Miguel Oks

Manufacturer

Drenttel Doyle Projects

Photographer

Seth Rubin

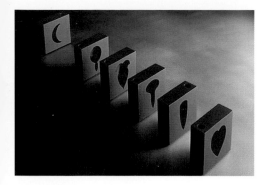

Product

Red Pictorial Plant Book

Caved out aluminum

flower vase.

Designer

Kazuo Kawaski

Manufacturer

Takata Lemnos Inc.

Photographer

Fujitsaka Mitsamasa

Product

Vase/Candle Holder

Can be used against wall

or as centerpiece.

Designer

Clodagh

Manufacturer

Architectural Sculpture

Associates

Photographer

Daniel Aubry

Product

Aluminum Candle Holder

Solid-stock aluminum, inspired

by minimalist geometric forms.

Designers

Miguel Oks

Stephen Doyle

Manufacturer

Drenttel Doyle Projects

Photographer

Seth Rubin

Product

Moon Candlestick

Sterling silver hand-forged disk

on oxidized bronze stand.

Designer

Ted Muehling

Manufacturer

Ted Muehling

Photographer

Dan Howell

Product

Tripod Candlestick

Horn disk and gold-leafed

pear wood on bronze stand.

Designer

Ted Muehling

Manufacturer

Ted Muehling

Photographer

Dan Howell

Product

Oxidized Bronze

Shell Dish

Designer

Ted Muehling

Manufacturer

Ted Muehling

Photographer

Dan Howell

Product

Horn Candlestick

Horn disk on oxidized

bronze stand.

Designer

Ted Muehling

Manufacturer

Ted Muehling

Photographer

Dan Howell

Product

Two Spoons

Sterling silver with black

and coral handles.

Designer

Ted Muehling

Manufacturer

Ted Muehling

Photographer

Dan Howell

Product
"David" Oil Lamp
Oil lamp with light reflector
and paraffin oil container.
Designer
Guido A. Niest
Manufacturer
Atelier Canaima, Italy
Photographer
Guido A. Niest

Product
Effigy Tray and Stand
Stainless steel tray and
aluminum stand.
Designers
Lisa Krohn
Martha Davis
Manufacturer
Alessi
Photographer
Lisa Krohn

Product
B/362 "Medusa" and
B/363 "Medea"
Réchaud and teapot.
Designer
Lino Sabattini
Manufacturer
Sabattini Argenteria S.p.A.
Photographer
Athos Lecce

Product

Spin™

Stackable flatware; large disks
at handle ends prevent jam-
ming in dishwasher baskets.

Designer

Linda Celentano

Manufacturer

Linda Celentano

Photographer

Linda Celentano

Product

Demi Lune

Stainless steel flatware.

Designers

**Sabina Müller,
Tino Melzer—
Melzer ID Konstanz**

Manufacturer

**Berndorf Luzern AG,
Luzern, Switzerland**

Photographer

Tino Melzer, Konstanz

Product

Farm Series

Four pots with hinged lids.

Designer

Montgomery/Pfeifer, Inc.

Manufacturer

WFM AG (Wurttemberg

ische Metallwaren Fabik)

Photographer

Dietmar Henneka,

Stuttgart,Germany

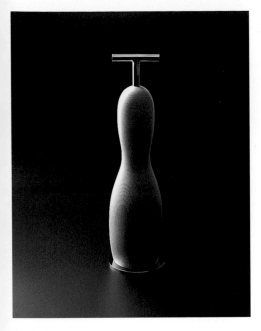

Product

"Jomfru Jensen"

Beech wood and stainless

steel pepper grinder.

Designer

Carsten Joergensen

Manufacturer

BODUM (Schweiz) AG

Photographer

BODUM (Schweiz) AG

Product

"Long Tall Sally"

Beech wood and stainless

steel salt and pepper grinder.

Designer

Carsten Joergensen

Manufacturer

BODUM (Schweiz) AG

Photographer

BODUM (Schweiz) AG

Product

"Nut-Max" Pepper Grinder

Beech wood and stainless

steel pepper grinder.

Designer

Carsten Joergensen

Manufacturer

BODUM (Schweiz) AG

Photographer

BODUM (Schweiz) AG

Product

"Peppino"

Beech wood and stainless

steel salt and pepper grinder.

Designer

Carsten Joergensen

Manufacturer

BODUM (Schweiz) AG

Photographer

BODUM (Schweiz) AG

As we make the transition from "worker bees" to "butterflies," products that enable us to make the most of our free time are increasingly important. Issues of safety, convenience, comfort, and fashion may begin to conflict with our biological need for adventure and excitement.

Designers must anticipate, understand, and analyze the dangers inherent in people's personal adventures but they must not design out those dangers. People need to understand the challenges and then they need equipment that keeps them on the edge of the experience.

Recreation

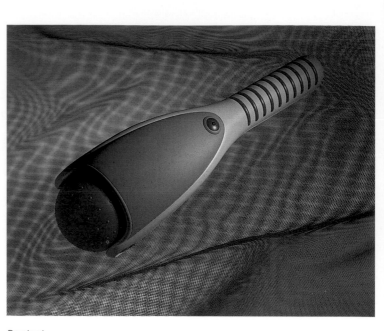

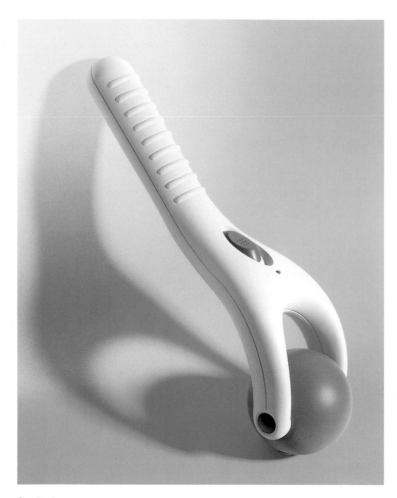

Product

Sports Massager with

Rotating Ball

Hand-held wand massager

with heat and variable speed.

Designers

Luc Heiligenstein,

Peter Langmar,

Richard Riback,

Stephen Melamed,

Francois Geneve—

Tres Design Group;

IDEO Engineering

Manufacturer

Sunbeam-Oster Household

Products, Schaumberg, IL

Photographer

Deborah Fletcher

Product

Ball Wand Massager

Less expensive hand-held

massager with rotating ball.

Designers

Luc Heiligenstein,

Peter Langmar,

Richard Riback,

Stephen Melamed,

Francois Geneve—

Tres Design Group;

IDEO Engineering

Manufacturer

Sunbeam-Oster Household

Products, Schaumberg, IL

Photographer

John Payne

Product

Ski Vertech and Alpine

Vertech Electronic Wrist

Instrument

Determines altitude using air-

craft altimeter technology.

Designers

Naoto Fukasawa,

Peter Spreenberg—

IDEO Product Development

Manufacturer

Avocet, Inc.

Photographer

Hidetoyo Sasaki

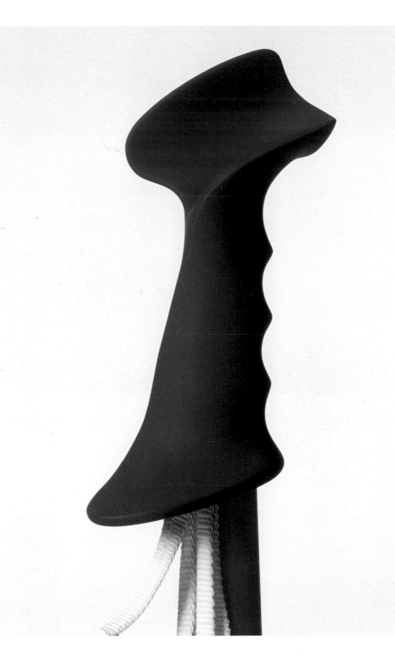

Product

Thumb-Sparing

Ski Pole Grip

Grip protects thumb

injuries while skiing.

Designer

Peter Stathis, principal,

Virtual Studio,

Cold Spring, NY

Manufacturer

MDesigns, New York, NY

Photographer

Peter Stathis

Product

Legacy Casting Reel

Lightweight reel for spin fishing.

Designers

Mark Stella,

Kuni Masuda,

Sohrab Vossoughi—

ZIBA Design Team

Manufacturer

Fenwick Inc.

Photographer

Michael Jones

Product

The Pump™ Shoe

Manual air system provides

adjustable, custom fit.

Designers

Andrew Jones, principal

industrial designer;

Carl Madore,

industrial designer;

David Chastain, principal

mechanical engineer;

Eric Cohen, senior

mechanical engineer—

Design Continuum Inc.

Manufacturer

Reebok International Ltd,

Stoughton, MA

Photographer

Design Continuum Inc.

Product

Airflex™ Glove

Flex points in glove pocket,

stretch areas in glove back

define glove's closing motion.

Designers

Andrew Jones, principal

industrial designer;

Carl Madore,

industrial designer;

David Chastain, principal

mechanical engineer

Harvey Koselka,

mechanical engineer—

Design Continuum Inc.

Manufacturer

Spalding Sports Worldwide,

Chicopee, Ma

Photographer

Design Continuum Inc.

Product

The Individual Trainer™

Computer estimates safe

fitness levels and develops

13 week workout programs.

Designers

Steve Wittenbrock,

Frank Friedman,

senior designers—

Soma, Inc.

Manufacturer

Leap, Inc.

Photographer

Steve Steckly

Product

Geoblade™ In-line Skate

Modular components provide

production cost savings

while preserving quality.

Designer

Michel Arney, principal

industrial designer,

Design Continuum Inc.

Manufacturer

Rollerblaade Inc.,

Minnetonka, MN

Photographer

Design Continuum Inc.

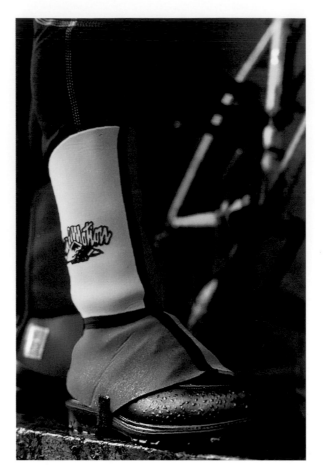

Product

Cycling Spats

Neoprene spats keep cyclist
dry and trousers clean.

Designer

Stuart Harvey Lee

Manufacturer

Local Motion, UK

Photographer

Stuart Harvey Lee

Product

**Orion All Weather
Photography Backpack**

Camera carrying system;
day pack, removable
fanny pack.

Designer

Doug Murdoch

Manufacturer

Lowe Pro International

Photographer

Halfmoon Photography

Product

Mountain bike light with

buzzer

Battery operated; fastens

easily to handlebar.

Designer

Shinobu Nakagawa

Manufacturer

Matsushita Battery

Industrial Co., Ltd.

Photographer

Matsushita Battery

Industrial Co., Ltd.

Product

Pro-Tec Adult/Youth

Bicycle Helmets

Three-dimensional surface

treatment accents styling

and venting patterns.

Designers

Jim Bergman, design director

Kevin Falk, senior designer

Bill Noble, designer

Manufacturer

Pro-Tec

Photographer

Rocky Salskov

Product

Spad Velco System

Designer

Frechin et Bureaux

Manufacturer

Research **for Le Cycle**

Photographer

Huyghe Veronique

Have you ever wondered why the telephone book doesn't have a miscellaneous section? It would probably be the most popular section—full of all the things that don't fit in other sections.

It's good to have things that don't fit into arbitrary categories. And it's really good to defy definition. Since randomness and doubt have become the basis of quantum physics and fractal mathematics, they certainly have an important role to play in good design.

Miscellaneous

Product

Project Ujima

African refugee support and

independence system.

Designer

Anthony Thaimu Ali Green

Manufacturer

Anthony Thaimu Ali Green

Photographer

Anthony Thaimu Ali Green

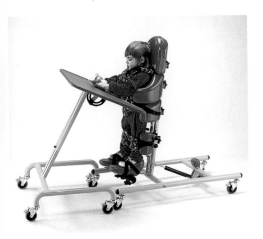

Product

Tri-Stander

Positions children in prone,

supine, or upright standing.

Designers

Kristine Wohnsen, project

manager; Samual Camardello,

product engineer; Elsie Bussey,

marketing research

Manufacturer

Tumble Forms of

Bissell Health Care

Photographer

Robert Kent

Product

Tadpole™

Pediatric infant positioning

system for children with

neuromuscular disorders.

Designers

Kristine Wohnsen

Michael Gravel, product

design manager

Photographer

G.R. Farley

Product

Anthropometric

Measuring System

Used by human factors spe-

cialists to take angular and lin-

ear measurements of body.

Designers

Steve Ward, senior

designer; Mark McLean,

Keith Shapland, designers

Manufacturer

Walter Dorwin Teague

Associates

Photographer

Jeff Curtis

Product
Adjustable Footrest
Footrest for office
workers adjusts easilly.
Designers
Robin Sarre, industrial design;
Jane Fulton, human factors;
Terry Christensen,
Julie Christensen—
mechanical engineering
Manufacturer
Details
Photographer
Henrik Kam

Product

Alesis QuardraSynth

Master Keyboard

Sixty-four-voice, 76-key

master keyboard for

music professionals.

Designers

Daniel Ashcraft, creative

director; Don Brown, pro-

ject designer; David

Benedetti, staff designer

Manufacturer

Alesis Corporation

Photographer

Tony Garcia

Product

Box of Paulownia wood.

Protects CDs, cassettes, and

photos from humidity.

Designers

Fumikazu Masuda

Hideya Kurosaki —

open house inc.

Manufacturer

Atsukawa Sangyo Co., Ltd.

Photographer

Kuniaki Okada

Product

1

Custom designed cosmetic
concept for the future would
incorporate all skin treatments.
Designers
David K. Peschel, D Product
James Gager, Prescriptives
Manufacturer
***Concept*, Prescriptives**
Photographers
Janet Beller
David K. Peschel

Product

GripIt

Ergonomic handle makes
carrying grocery/shopping
bags comfortable.
Designers
Song Kee Hong,
Kim Porter,
Sohrab Vossoughi—
ZIBA Design Team
Manufacturer
Yaji International, Inc.
Photographer
Michael Jones

Product

Credit Card Cash Clip

Uses expired product
in new way.
Designer
David K. Peschel,
D Product
Manufacturer
D Product
Photographers
Janet Beller
David K. Peschel

Product

Elektra

Entertainment Watch

Shows 19 cities in 5 time zones.
Designer
Stephen Doyle, art director;
Mats Hakanson, designer—
Drenttel Doyle Partners
Manufacturer
Bulova
Photographer
Drenttel Doyle Partners

Product

"Words for Weary

Designers"

Folded paper system gives
solace/inspiration to designer.
Designer
Beth Mosher
Manufacturer
Gallery 91
Photographer
Beth Mosher

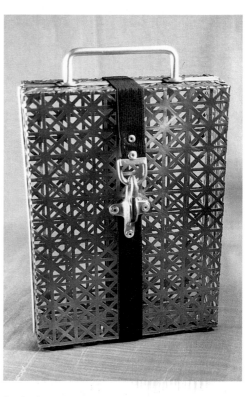

Product

Messenger Bag

Made of Italian calfskin.

Designer

Krohn Design

Manufacturer

Prototype

Photographers

Lisa Krohn

Tucker Viemeister

Product

Overnight bag

Made of Italian calfskin.

Designer

Krohn Design

Manufacturer

Prototype

Photographers

Lisa Krohn

Tucker Viemeister

Product

Portfolio Case SM

Carrying case for designers

and photographers.

Designer

David Weeks

Photographer

David Weeks

Product

Silhouette Trend

Collection "Minimal Art"

Mod. 9708

Lightweight eyeglasses

with hinge-free frames.

Designer

Gerhard Fuchs, Silhouette

Manufacturer

Silhouette International

GmbH

Photographer

Silhouette Advertising

Department

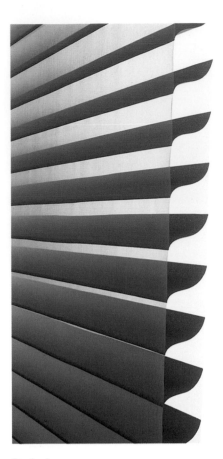

Product

Silhouette® Window Shadings

Combine best elements of
shades, blinds and curtains
into single treatment.

Designers

**Wendell Colson, design
principal; Paul Swiszcz;
Joe Kovach; Terry Akins**

Manufacturer

**Hunter Douglas Window
Fashions Division**

Photographer

**Hunter Douglas Window
Fashions**

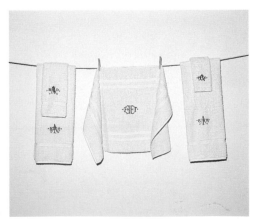

Product

What's What Towels

Labeled face, hand, bath,
and feet in monograms.

Designers

**Marco Pasanella
Alexander Brebner**

Manufacturer

The Pasanella Company

Photographer

Kit Latham

Product

Halley

Marble tile inlay work in
Portuguese pink, pearl gray.

Designer

Roberto Marcatti

Manufacturer

UP & UP srl

Photographer

Programma Immagine

Product

Stainless Steel Frame

Provides elegant transition
from wall to the art.

Designer

Miguel Oks

Manufacturer

Drenttel Doyle Projects

Photographer

Seth Rubin

Product

Modular Post Box System

Durable mailboxes with interior
containers for less mail damage.

Designers

Karim Rashid

Kan Industrial Design

Manufacturer

Canada Post Corporation,

Canada

Photographer

Doug Hall

Product

Sealed Lever Latch

Trigger release adjustable
lever latch fastener.

Designers

Gabriel Gromotka

Peter Bressler

Manufacturer

Southco, Inc.

Photographer

Stephen Mullen

Photography

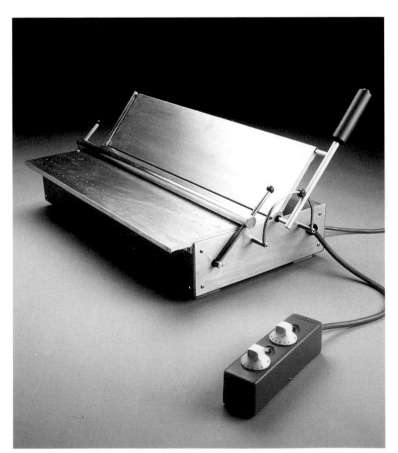

Product

Effective Acrylic Sheet
Bending Device

Inexpensive, accurate device
allows bending angle to be
monitored and adjusted.

Designer

Vincent Shum Yiu Man

Manufacturer

Vincent Shum Yiu Man

Photographer

Vincent Shum Yiu Man

Product

**Thetascan Precision Laser
Measurement Instrument**

Instrument used for the precise
measurement of angles.

Designers

**Jay Wilson, industrial
designer; Ted Bryant,
mechanical designer—
GVO Inc.**

Manufacturer

Micro-Radian, Can Maecos, CA

Photographer

Kelley King

In the past, all industrial design curriculums were derived from either the German Bauhaus or Pratt Institute models. Schools from Finland to Japan basically offered the same study program as schools in San Francisco or Kansas City. Nowadays, different schools have developed their own approaches and their own personalities, and these are reflected in their students' work.

Education has shifted away from vocational training to critical thinking, creative development, research, and environmental leadership. Similar to other professional schools, design schools are incubating and exploring issues significant to society as a whole and the design profession specifically.

Although this is by no means a comprehensive collection of student work, it is a good overview of what's going on in design schools.

Design Schools

Product
Cruiser Commuter
Motorcycle modernizes style
of classic Harley Davidson.
Designer
Al Arrosagaray
Photographer
Steven A. Heller

Product
Recumbent Motorcycle
Small wheels descend when
traveling at low speeds.
Designer
Robert Laster
Photographer
Steven A. Heller

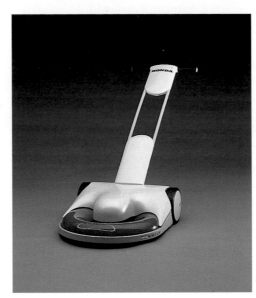

Product
Baby Stroller
Round protective shell
ejects when struck.
Designer
Dani Santacreu
Photographer
Steven A. Heller

Product
Orbit Lawnmower
Whirling blades guided by
magnetic levitation system.
Designer
Dan Vehse
Photographer
Steven A. Heller

Product
Moonbeam
Home audio/video system.
Designers
Hsin-Chien Huang, James Lee
Photographer
Steven A. Heller

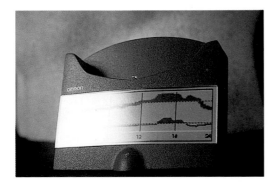

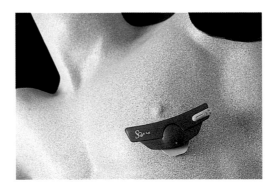

Product
**Compact Vital Signs
Monitoring Device**
Monitors blood pressure, pulse,
temperature, cardiac output.
Designer
Brian Channell
Photographer
Steven A. Heller

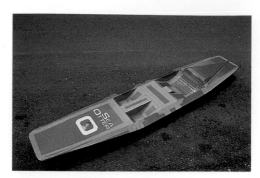

Product
Cardboard Kayak
Designer
Robert Donovan
Photographer
Richard Britnell

Product
Cardboard Kayak
Designer
David Stoddard
Photographer
Richard Britnell

Products
Cardboard Kayak Class Photo
Designer
Richard Britnell
Photographer
Clark Lundell

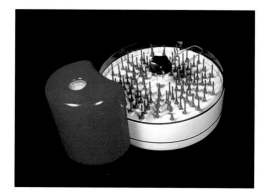

Product
Syringe Carousel
Designer
Randy Bernard
Photographer
Randy Bernard

Product
NASA Lunar Rover
Designers
Jack Lallor, David Hobbs
Steve Zwonitzer, Jim Catoe
Photographers
David Hobbs, Steve Zwonitzer

Product
NASA Lunar Cargo Lander
and Off Loading Vehicle
Designers
Stacey Aderholt, Charles Baker
Photographer
Stacey Aderholt

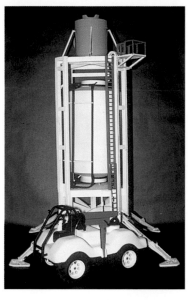

Product
Portable Hair Dryer
Designer
Bruce Lee
Photographer
Bruce Lee

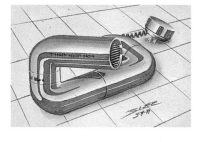

Product
"Telecomfax"
Transportable office
telecommunications.
Designer
Richard Britnell
Photographer
John Oliver

Product
Peak 10 Camp Stove
Two-burner camp stove.
Designer
Brett Ritter
Photographer
Brett Ritter

Product
Hikers Pack
Hiking pack assembles easily
into lightweight chair.
Designer
David Klausner
Photographers
Kislip Ongchango, David Klausner

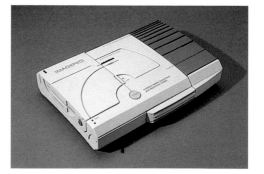

Product
ImagePro
Two-dimensional visual image
collecting/presenting system.
Designer
David Peng
Photographer
David Peng

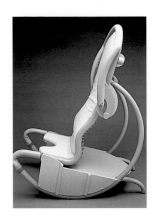

SIVA SEAT FRONT ELEV. - 50.0% USER

SIVA SEAT - LAYING ELEV. - 50.0% USER

SIVA SEAT - EMERGENCY [TRENDELENBURG] ELEV. - 50.0% USER

Product
Siva Seat
Adjustable support system
for labor and delivery.
Designer
Laura Caghan
Photographer
Victoria Damrel

Product
**Aequus Diabetes
Self-Care System**
Convenient self-care
system for diabetics.
Designer
Edward Mitchell
Photographer
Edward Mitchell

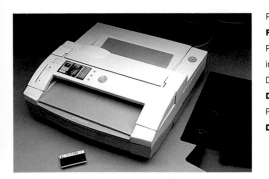

Product
FilmFax
Proposes new capabilities
in patient diagnostics.
Designer
David Klausner
Photographer
David Klausner

Product
Water Fountain
Designer
Tyler R. Berkheiser
Photographer
Tyler R. Berkheiser

Product
Towel Dispenser/Hand Dryer
Combination
Designer
Michael Arajakis
Photographer
Michael Arajakis

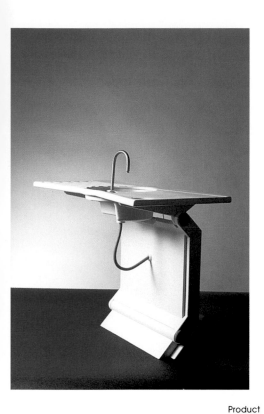

Product
Universal Kitchen
Designer
Vanessa Sica
Sponsor
Whirlpool
Photographer
Vanessa Sica

Product
Accessible Restroom for
Railroad Cars
Designers
Ken Coleman,
Jennifer Gaspari, Kerry Mellor
Sponsor
Amtrak
Photographers
Ken Coleman,
Jennifer Gaspari, Kerry Mellor

Product
Table Fan
Designer
Jeffrey F. Miller
Photographer
Jeffrey F. Miller

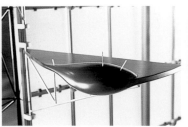
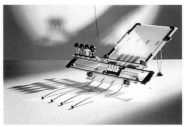

Product
Electronic Workstation
Designers
Brian Kritzman
Carol Lasch

Product
Ithaca Solid Ink Color Printer
Exposed interior elements
express function.
Designer
Donald Carr
Sponsor
NCR Corporation
Photographer
Tom Wedell

Product
Computer
Designer
Bill Wurz

Product
Drive-Up Phone
Designer
Eric Williams
Sponsor
NYNEX

Product
Celestial Navigator
Designer
Brian Kritzman

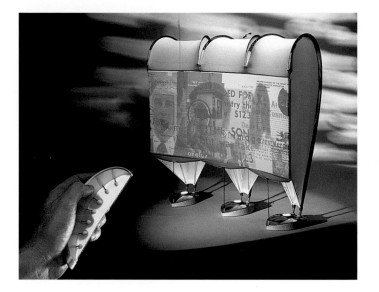

Product
Nomadic Workstation
Imagery can be manipulated by
combining voice with gesture.
Designer
Donald Carr
Sponsor
NCR Corporation
Photographer
C. Clor

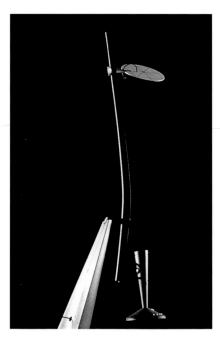

Product
Computer Projector
Designer
Masamichi Udagawa

Product
Skull Glove
Integrated swimmer's
cap and goggles.
Designer
Unaiza Shaikh
Photographer
Bobby Hansson

Product
"Spandance"
Stretchable lycra
aerobic outfit.
Designer
Allstone Charles
Photographer
Bobby Hansson

Product
"Buggin"
Child's safety helmet.
Designer
Kevin Owen
Photographer
Bobby Hansson

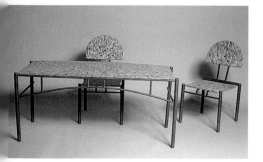

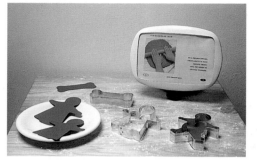

Product
School Furniture
Recycled plastic familiarizes
children with recycling.
Designer
Stanley Stewart, III
Photographer
Bobby Hansson

Product
Electronic Cookbook
Electronic cookbook with
touch-sensitive screen.
Designer
Mari Ando
Photographer
Bobby Hansson

Product
Face Phone
Face phone with
viewing option.
Designer
Robert Story
Photographer
Bobby Hansson

Product
Roller Bearings
Roller blades with 9 ball bearings.
Designer
Joseph Puma
Photographer
Bobby Hansson

Product
Hide Away Bed
Child's bed with crawling space,
peepholes and toy storage.
Designer
Lori Johnson
Photographer
Bobby Hansson

Product
Computerized Devices
Designer
Clarence Feng
Photographer
Clarence Feng

Product
Dinnerware/Tea Setting
Designer
Anne Topaj
Photographer
Anne Topaj

Product
Mammography Imaging Device
Designer
Jane Saks Cohan
Photographer
Jane Saks Cohan

Product
Airport Passenger Check-In
Designer
Charles T. Bender
Photographer
Charles T. Bender

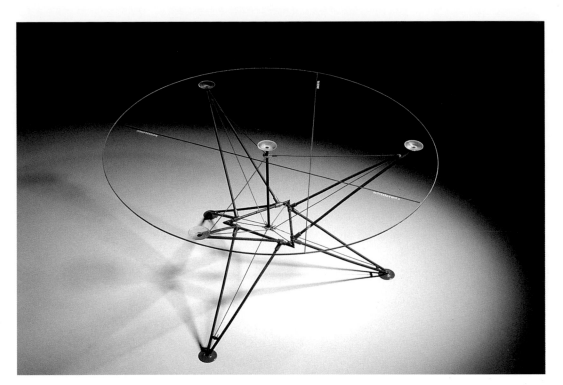

Product
Table
Designer
Giovanni Pellone
Photographer
Giovanni Pellone

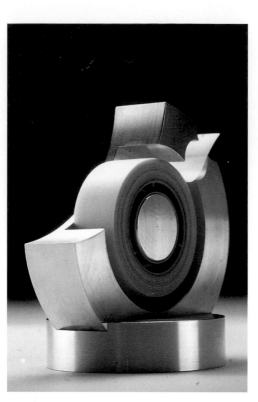

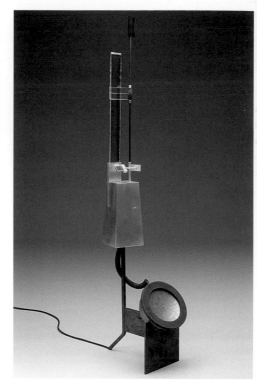

Product
"Slicky"
Recycled products project.
Designer
David Clarke

Product
Tape Dispenser
Designer
Metals 1 Class

Product
Radio
Resists typical radio design.
Designer
John F. Wells
Photographer
Tod Babick

Product
Tea Set for a Mass Murderer
Bronze and copper tea set.
Designer
Philip Crangi
Photographer
Philip Crangi

Product
Voice Modulator
Study of voice
recognition computing.
Designer
Jan-Christoph Zoels
Photographer
Spencer Ladd

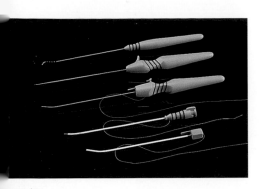

Product
Laparoscopic Knee Surgery
Instrument System
Designers
Richard Kervel, Beth Maccaroni
Heather Rentz, Jerome Tomaselli

Product
Stretch Fabric Chair
Designer
John Bozak

Product
Pneumatic Nailer/Compressor
and Handling Project
Designers
Jonathon Hayes, Tamera Crawford
Ivan Brewster, David Gomez-Rosado

Product
Bob-Ono
Vehicle; front module is
allowed lateral rotation.
Designer
Reynold Rodriguez
Sponsor
Nissan
Photographers
Peter Kelly, Reynold Rodriguez

Product
Racing Wheelchair
Ninety-one pound carbon
filter racing wheelchair.
Designer
Richard Trumble

Product
Wood & Steel Chair
Designer
Christopher Martin

Product
Kinetic Luminaire
Ceiling-mounted lighting device.
Designer
Tod Babick
Photographer
Tod Babick

Product

Sports Camera

For high speed sports
photography.

Designers

Jason A. Clark, Thomas Corlett

Sponsor

Polaroid

Photographer

Thomas Corlett

Product
Full Suspension Mountain Bike
With rubber dampening system.
Designers
Christopher Carter
Leo Gonzales, Tom Marquis
Sponsor
Marin Bicycles, San Rafael, CA
Photographer
Tom Marquis

Product
Tuki: A Future Memory Amplifier
Reads mind and provides
additional memory.
Designer
Eyal Eliav
Photographer
Eyal Eliav

Product
Wrist Watch Study
Injection molded clear case
improves water resistance.
Designers
Michael Garman, Thomas Yeh
Sponsor
Timex Corporation
Photographer
Michael Garman

Product
Henry: The Expanding,
Contracting Jug
Rubber bladder supported
by steel wires.
Designer
Jacqueline Wilkinson
Photographer
Jacqueline Wilkinson

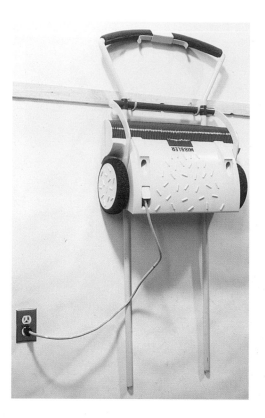

Product

"Nibbler"

Rechargeable electric

lawn mower/mulcher.

Designers

Douglas J. Carpiaux

James McCormick

Photographer

Douglas J. Carpiaux

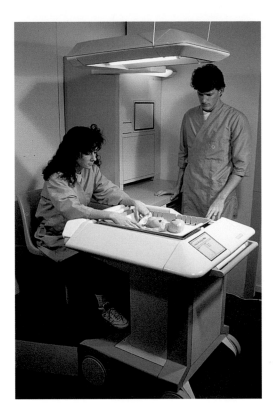

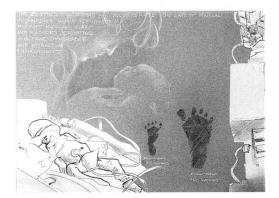

Product

Sanctuary

System for neonatal care.

Designer

Richard Walters

Photographer

Richard Walters

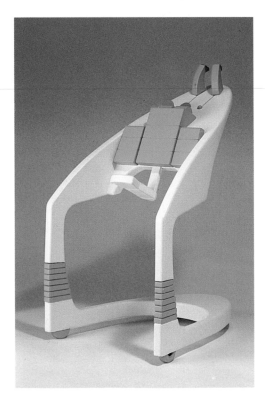

Product

Phoenix

Walking device.

Designer

Paul D. Rothstein

Photographer

Paul D. Rothstein

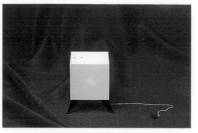

Les Ateliers

Product

Radios

Three radios with similar form, but
different significances
and definitions.

Designer

Chi-Wing Lee

Photographer

Huyghe Veronique

Les Ateliers

Product

Archi-

Telephone/answering machine.

Designer

Chi-Wing Lee

Photographer

Huyghe Veronique

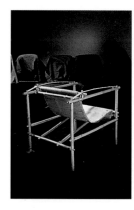

Les Ateliers

Product

Rose

Lighting device creates
candle-light effect.

Designer

Chi-Wing Lee

Photographer

Huyghe Veronique

College of Art and Design

Product

Future Generation ATM

For banking, travel arrangements,
electronic shopping.

Designer

Robert Fitzpatrick

Sponsor

NCR Corporation

Photographer

Alexander, Glass, Ingersol Inc.

Domus Academy, Milan

Product

The Tranquil Line

Grocery line concept for the
future minimizes inconvenience.

Designer

Brian Jablonski

Photographer

Brian Jablonski

**Hong Kong Polytechnic,
Swire School of Design**

Product

Bamboo Chair

Flexible jointing method
facilitates mass-production.

Designer

Chi-Wing Lee

Photographer

Conrad Pong

**The Academy of Fine Arts,
Hamburg, Germany**

Product

Electric Bicycle

Auxiliary engine in front wheel
supports pedal movement.

Designers

Hilams Jaedicke

Gerd Schmieta, Mathias Seiler

Photographer

Bernd Ebsen

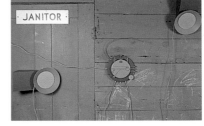

**Milwaukee Institute
of Art and Design**
Product
Spinal Cord Injury
Patient Prone Cart
Hydraulic leveling system allows
multi-position adjustment.
Designers
Todd Hoehn
Robert Meurer, Sam Schnurr
Photographer
C.J. Zablocki, VA Medical Center

University of Illinois
Product
Tape Player with Radio
Tape and radio placed
on central knob.
Designer
Beth Mosher
Photographers
Beth Mosher
Rick Loduha

University of Illinois
Product
Gingko Chair
Stacking chair utilizes the flexibility
of polypropylene.
Designer
Beth Mosher
Photographer
Beth Mosher

**Wellington Polytechnic School
of Design, New Zealand**
Product
P.P.U.
Portable Presentation Unit
For photographers and designers.
Designer
Jarrod Lane-Linton
Photographer
Jarrod Lane-Linton

**Wellington Polytechnic School
of Design, New Zealand**
Product
Vehemence
Designer
Jarrod Lane-Linton
Photographer
Jarrod Lane-Linton

Appendix

DESIGNERS/MANUFACTURERS

Able Design, Inc.
54 West 21st Street, Suite 705
New York, NY 10010

Harry Allen
67 East Second Street, #20
New York, NY 10003

Alps OEM Group
3553 North First Street
San Jose, CA 95134

Annie Walwyn-Jones Ltd.
40 West 37th Street
New York, NY 10018

Apple Computer, Inc.
20525 Mariani Avenue
Cupertino, CA 95014

Apple Computer, Inc.
20730 Valley Green Drive, MS-65ID
Cupertino, CA 95014

Arkkit Forms Design
692A Moulton Avenue
Los Angeles, CA 90031

Daniel Ashcraft
Ashcraft Design
11832 West Pico Boulevard
Los Angeles, CA 90064

Atelier Canaima
Vaile Kennedy 10
22070 Bregnano/Como, Italy

Axis Group
65 Bellwoods Avenue
Toronto, Ontario, Canada

Tod Babick
181 Pleasant Street
Providence, RI 02906

Bissell Healthcare Corporation
J.A. Preston Division
PO Box 89
744 West Michigan Avenue
Jackson, MI 49204

Bissell Inc.
2345 Walker Road NW
Grand Rapids, MI 49504

Black & Decker - Housewares
6 Armstrong Road
Shelton, CT 06484

Bodum (Schweiz) AG
Kantonsstrasse
6234 Triengen, Switzerland

The Boeing Airplane Co.
PO Box 3707
M/S 02-JM
Seattle, WA 98124

Constantin Boym
Boym Design Studio
56 West 11th Street
New York, NY 10011

Shashi B. Caan
423 Clinton Avenue
Brooklyn, NY 11238

Laura Caghan
Industrial Strength Design
17282 Whetmore
Huntington Beach, CA 92647

Linda Celentano
555 B Shaler Blvd.
Ridgefield, NJ 07657

Christine Van Der Hurd, Inc.
99 University Place, 9th floor
New York, NY 10003

Clodagh Design International
365 1st Avenue
New York, NY 10010

Chris Collicott
1151½ North La Brea Avenue
Los Angeles, CA 90038

Comme des Garcons
12 West 57th Street, #903
New York, NY 10019

Philip Crangi
171 Chestnut Street
Providence, RI 02903

D Product
325 West 13th Street, 4th Floor
New York, NY 10014

Dakota Jackson Inc.
306 East 61st Street
New York, NY 10021

Data General Corp.
4400 Computer Drive
Westboco, MA 01580

Design Continuum Inc.
648 Beacon Street
Boston, MA 02215

Design Form Technik AG
Hofi 501, FL-9497
Triesenberg, Liechtenstein

Designspring, Inc.
60 Post Road West
Westport, CT 06880

Dictaphone Industrial Group
Dictaphone Corporation
3191 Broadbridge Avenue
Stratford, CT 06497

Digital Equipment Corp.
146 Main Street
Maynard, MA 01754

Drenttel Doyle Partners
1123 Broadway
New York, NY 10010

Ebemistene Luthy SA
22 Rue Marzioni
1227 Geneva, Switzerland

Ecart International
111 Rue Saint Antoine
7504 Paris, France

ERCO Leuchten GmbH
Postfach 2460
D-5880 Ludenscheid, Germany

Flip Design
51 MacDougal Street #157
New York, NY 10012

Flos Spa
Via Angela Faini 2
25073 Bovezzo Brescia, Italy

Frechin & Bureaux
38 Rue Croix Des Petits Champs
75001 Paris, France

frogdesign inc.
4600 Bohannon Drive, # 101
Menlo Park, CA 94025

The Gillette Company
Prudential Tower Building
Boston, MA 02199

Christopher Graziano
Graziano Mosaics
154 Stanton Street
New York, NY 10002

Anthony Thaimu Ali Green
209 Harvard Street
Boston, MA 02124

Green Design Inc.
7 South Street, PO Box 908
Yarmouth, ME 04096

Pascal Grossiord
28 Rue Roolier
75009 Paris, France

Group Four Design
147 Simsbury Road
Avon, CT 06001

GVO, Inc.
2370 Watson Court
Palo Alto, CA 94303

Hewlett-Packard Company
700 71st Avenue
Greeley, CO 80634

Hewlett-Packard Company
1266 Kifer Road
Sunnyvale, CA 94086

Todd Hoehn
1825 East Lafayette Place, Apartment R
Milwaukee, WI 53207

James M. Howard
Howard Design Inc.
3155 Route 10 East, #214
Denville, NJ 07834

Hunter Douglas Windows Fashions
2 Park Way & Route 17 South
Upper Saddle River, NJ 07458

IBM Corporation
9000 South Rita Road
Tucson, AZ 85744

IDEO Product Development
7/8 Jeffreys Place
Jeffreys Place
London NW1 9PP, England

IDEO Product Development
1527 Stockton Street, 4th Floor
San Francisco, CA 94133

IDEO Product Development
660 High Street
Palo Alto, CA 94301

Brian Jablonski
31302 Churchill Drive
Birmingham, MI 48009

Kazuo Kawasaki
Kazuo Kawasaki Design Room
2-40-10, Nitazuka
Fukui, 910, Japan

David Klausner
12629 Killion Street
North Hollywood, CA 91607

The Knoll Group
105 Wooster Street
New York, NY 10012

The Knoll Group
655 Madison Avenue
New York, NY 10021

Krohn Design
2348 Loma Vista Place
Los Angeles, CA 90039

Dietz Design Management GmbH
Scheffelstrasse 5
D-60318 Frankfurt, Germany

labIntelligence
191 Jefferson Avenue
Menlo Park, CA 94025

Jarrod Lane-Linton
c/o Smart Design Inc.
7 West 18th Street, 8th Floor
New York, NY 10011

Lara Designs Inc.
7355 Northwest 54 Court
Fort Lauderdale, FL 33319

Larsen Design Studio
41 East 11th Street, 9th Floor
New York, Ny 10003

LD Yamagiwa Laboratory Ltd.
5-18 Higashinippori 4-Chome Arakawa-ku
Tokyo, 116, Japan

Chi-Wing Lee
A3, 20 Rue Des Annelets
75019 Paris, France

Stuart Harvey Lee
#6D, 29 Avenue B
New York, NY 10009

Laurene Leon
56 West 11th Street
New York, NY 10011

Lunar Design
537 Hamilton Avenue
Palo Alto, CA 94301

Pascal Luthy
Maison Dupin SA
Rue Du Rhône 11
1211 Geneva 24, Switzerland

Machen Montague, Inc.
2221 Edge Lake Drive, Suite #100
Charlotte, NC 28217

Vincent Shum Yiu Man
Lasalle-Sia A College of the Arts
Lorong J, Telok Kurau Road
Singapore 1542

Roberto Marcatti
Roberto Marcatti Architecto
Via Magolfa 13
20143 Milan, Italy

Carl Martinez
520 East 14th Street #18
New York, NY 10009

Matsushita Battery Industrial Co.
2 Matsushita-cho Morieuchi
Osaka, 570, Japan

Matsushita Electric Industrial Co., Ltd.
2-2-8 Hinode-cho, Toyonaka
Osaka, 7561, Japan

Matsushita Electric Industrial Co., Ltd.
1-15, Matsuo-cho, Kadoma-city
Osaka, 571, Japan

Matsushita Kotobuki Electronics
Industries Ltd.
247 Fukutake, Saijo
Ehime, 793, Japan

Matsushita Seiko Co., Ltd.
61-2-6 Chome, Imafukunishi, Joto-ku
Osaka City, 536, Japan

Ingo Maurer GmbH
Kaiserstrasse 47
80801 Munich, Germany

McBrayer Industrial Design
PO Box 310186
New Braunfels, TX 78131

Medin Corporation
111 Lester Street
Wallington, NJ 07057

Melzer ID
Blarerstrasse 56
7750 Konstanz, Germany

Edward D. Mitchell
524 Coronado Avenue, Apt. #13
Long Beach, CA 90814

Molecular Dynamics
880 Arques Avenue
Sunnyvale, CA 94086

Montgomery/Pfeifer, Inc.
461 Bush Street #230
San Francisco, CA 94108

Beth Mosher
700 Taylor Street, #404
San Francisco, CA 94108

Ted Muehling
47 Greene Street
New York, NY 10013

Doug Murdoch
Fluxion Design Genesis
2190 Northpoint Parkway
Santa Rosa, CA 95407

NCR Canada Ltd.
580 Weber Street North
Waterloo, Ontario N2J4G5, Canada

NCR Corporation
1700 South Patterson Blvd.
Dayton, OH 45479

NOTO S.R.L.
Via Vigevano 8
20144 Milan, Italy

Novodesign
Av. Infante Santo 69
1400 Lisboa, Portugal

NUNO Corporation
B1 Axis 5-17-1
Roppongi, Minato-ku
Tokyo, 106, Japan

open house inc.
Forum Building
1-28-13 Hamamatsucho Minatoku
Tokyo, 105, Japan

Palo Alto Design Group
360 University Avenue
Palo Alto, CA 94301

Lunar Design Inc.
537 Hamilton Avenue
Palo Alto, CA 94301

Park Scientific Instruments
1171 Borregas Avenue
Sunnyvale, CA 94089

The Pasanella Company
45 West 18th Street, 7th Floor
New York, NY 10011

Palo Pedrizzetti
Palo Pedrizzetti & Assoc.
Via Adige 6
20135 Milan, Italy

David Peng
2022 West Niore Avenue
Anaheim, CA 92804

Perry Design, Inc.
121 West 3rd Street
New York, NY 10012

Product Insight Inc.
6 Ledgerock Way, Unit 1
Acton, MA 01720

Punt Mobles, S.L.
Islas Baledres
48-P.I. Fuente Del Jarro
46980 Paterma, Spain

Karim Rashid
Karim Rashid Industrial Design
145 West 27th Street
New York, NY 10001

Resolute
1013 Stewart Street
Seattle, WA 98101

Brett Ritter
925 Coastline Drive
Seal Beach, CA 90740

Reynold Rodriguez
Box 4343
Old San Juan, Puerto Rico

Michael Rowe
401½ Workshop
401½ Wandsworth Road
London SW8 2JP, England

Ryobi America Corp.
5201 Pearman Dairy Road
Anderson, SC 29625

S.G. Hauser Associates Inc.
24009 Ventura Boulevard, Suite #200
Calabasas, CA 91302

Sabatini Argenteria SpA
Via Don Capiaghi 2
22070 Bregnano/Como, Italy

Hidetoyo Sasaki
6-4-11-26 Akasaka Minatoku
Tokyo, Japan

Winfried Scheuer
53 Leinster Square
London, England

Udo Schill
Beyond Design
3-19-4-303 Shimo Meguro-ku
Tokyo, 153, Japan

Mathais Seiler
Susannenster 36
D-2000 Hamburg 36, Germany

Silhouette International GmbH
Ellbognerstrasse 24, Postfach 538
A-4021 Linz, Austria

Smart Design Inc.
7 West 18th Street
New York, NY 10011

Soma, Inc.
514 NW 11th Avenue, #209
Portland, OR 97209

Sony Corporation
1 Sony Drive, Mail Drop 1D6
Park Ridge, NJ 07656

Southco, Inc.
210 North Brinton Lake Road
Concordville, PA 19331

Steiner Design Associates
214 Pemberwick Road
Greenwich, CT 06831

Frank Sterpka
Island Design
153 Brace Road
West Hartford, CT 06107

Steuben
717 Fifth Avenue
New York, NY 10022

Studio/Ricchio
PO Box 3028
Seal Beach, CA 90740

Tres Design Group
1440 North Dayton Street
Chicago, IL 60622

TZ Design
122 Washington Avenue
Brooklyn, NY 11205

Fernd Van Engelen
15413 Southeast 46 Place
Bellevue, WA 98006

Marc Van Hoe
N.V. Van Hoe
Grote Heerweg 35
8791 Beveren-Leie, Belgium

Virtual Studio
15 Academy Street
Cold Spring, NY 10516

Stacy Walsh
338 East 22nd Street
New York, NY 10010

Walter Dorwin Teague Associates
14727 NE 87th Street
Redmond, WA 98557

David Weeks
377A Atlantic Avenue, #2
Brooklyn, NY 11217

John F. Wells
Phenomena
335 Northwest 50th Street
Seattle, WA 98107

Zanotta SpA
Via Vittorio Veneta 57
20054 Milan, Italy

ZIBA Design
305 West 21st Avenue
Portland, OR 97209

Ziggurat
419 West G Street
San Diego, CA 92101

Jan-Christoph Zoels
426 Benefit Street
Providence, RI 02903

DESIGN SCHOOLS
Art Center College of Design
1700 Lida Street
Pasadena, CA 91103

Auburn University
Department Industrial Design
O.D. Smith Hall, Room #103
Auburn, AL 36849

California State University, Long Beach
1250 Bellflower
Long Beach, CA 90815

Carnegie Mellon
Department of Design
110 Margaret Morrison
Pittsburgh, PA 15213

Cranbrook Academy of Art
Box 801
Bloomfield Hills, MI 48303

Parsons School of Design
Product Design Department
66 Fifth avenue
New York, NY 10011

Pratt Institute
200 Willoughby Avenue
Brooklyn, NY 11205

Rhode Island School of Design
2 College Street
Providence, RI 02903

The University of the Arts
320 South Broad Street
Philadelphia, PA 19102

University of Wisconsin, Stout
Menominee, WI 54751-0790

PHOTOGRAPHERS

Joe Atlas
Atlas Photography
1308 Factory Place, Studio #33
Los Angeles, CA 90013

Alexander Bayer
Vision Fotostudio AG
Hauptstrasse 29
CH-9436 Balgach, Switzerland

James Beard
45 Richmond Road
Providence, RI 02903

Janet Beller
225 Varick
New York, NY 10014

Giampiero Benvenuti
1655 Polk Street
San Francisco, CA 94108

Copyline Corp.
40 West 37th Street, 4th floor
New York, NY 10018

David Cripps
10 Amwell Street
London, England

Victoria Damrel
4752 Pearce Avenue
Long Beach, CA 90808

Ric Deliantoni
C & I Photography
275 Santa Anna Court
Sunnyvale, CA 94086

Liz Deschenes
237 Lafayette Street, #8W
New York, NY 10012

Horst Eifert
Team Photo Ulm
2 Heinkelstr
7900 Ulm, Germany

Rick English Photography
1162 Bryant
San Francisco, CA 94103

Deborah Fletcher
1744 West Grand
Chicago, IL 60622

Tony Garcia
Tony Garcia Photography
5245 Melrose Avenue
Los Angeles, CA 90038

Mark Gottlieb
1915 University Avenue
East Palo Alto, CA 94303

Rob Gray
160 West End Avenue
New York, NY 10023

Tom Del Guercio
5 River Road
Little Falls, NJ 07424

Giorgio Gugnani
Via Serbelloni-1
Milan, Italy

Halfmoon Photography
2224 Northport Parkway
Santa Rosa, CA 95407

Doug Hall
629 Eastern Avenue
Toronto, Ontario, Canada

Jeffrey Muir Hamilton
6719 North Quartzite Canyon
Tucson, AZ 85718

Dietmar Henneka
24 Moerikestr
70178 Stuttgart, Germany

Bernd Hoff
45147 Essen
8 Virchowstz, Germany

Ed Horrigan
67 Great Road
Maynard, MA 01754

Dan Howell
160 Fifth Avenue, #718
New York, NY 10011

Michael B. Hussey, Jr.
3210 Piper's Way
High Point, NC 27265

Charles Impstepf
Charles Imstepf Studios
620 Moulton Avenue, Studio 216
Los Angeles, CA 90031

Junichi Kaizuka
101, 2-5-8 Honmachi, Hoyashi
Tokyo, 202, Japan

Henrik Kam
2325 3rd Street, #408
San Francisco, CA 94107

Karant & Asssociates, Inc.
400 North May Street
Chicago, IL 60622

Miles Keep
3392 Saint Michael Drive
Palo Alto, CA 94301

Charles Kemper
762 Clementica
San Francisco, CA 94103

Kelley King Photography
441 East Columbine Avenue, Suite D
Santa Ana, CA 92707

Steve Knight
Steve Knight Photography
1212 East 10th Street
Charlotte, NC 28204

Spencer Ladd
29 Humbolt Avenue
Providence, RI 02906

Dan Langley
911 East Pike Street
Seattle, WA 98122

Kit Latham
1225 Park Avenue, #4D
New York, NY 10128

Rick Loduha
610 Wilson, #5
Lafayette, LA 70503

Jonathan Mankin
2216 Bismarck Court
Loveland, CO 80538

Tracy Maurer
Tracy Maurer Photography
315 Ninth Street, Suite 2
San Antonio, TX 78215

Sue McNab
3-21-12, Eifuku, Suginami-ku
Tokyo, 168, Japan

Fujitsaka Mitsamasa
5-3 Minamimotomachi
Shinjuku-Ku
Tokyo, Japan

Stan Musliek
2141 3rd Street
San Francisco, CA 94107

Geoffrey Nelson
2235-C Old Middlefield Way
Mountain View, CA 94043

Kuniaki Okada
5-19-9 Higashinakano, Nakanoku
Tokyo, 164, Japan

Omega Studios Inc.
PO Box 780
High Point, NC 27261

Peter Orkin
12 South Main Street
South Norwalk, CT 06854

John Parsekian
5 Lawrence Street, Building #15
Bloomfield, NJ 07003

John Payne
John Payne Photo Ltd.
2250 West Grand Ave
Chicago, IL 60612

Keith Piacesny
56 West 11th Street, #9FW
New York, NY 10011

Conrad Pong
6/F Pennington Commercial Bldg.
17 Pennington Street
Causeway Bay, Hong Kong

Michael Pruzan
28 Washington Avenue
Morganville, NJ 07751

Marino Ramazzotti
Via Luogo Pio 7, Muggio
Milan, Italy

David H. Ramsey
1124 South Mint Street
Charlotte, NC 28203

Steve Robb
535 Albany Street
Boston, MA 02118

Robert Moore Photography
92 Van Dam Street, #4
New York, NY 10013

Seth Rubin
305 East 10th Street, #3
New York, NY 10009

Rocky Salskov
1115 East Street
Seattle, WA 98122

Masumi Sato
201 Ishii Bld. , 3-Banchi
Katamachi, Shinjuku-ku
Tokyo, 160, Japan

Bjorn Schulze
1280 West Peachtree St., NW, #1512
Atlanta, GA 30367

Stephen Mullen Photography
825 North Second Street
Philadelphia, PA 19123

John Stuart
80 Varick Street, #8E
New York, NY 10013

Terry Sutherland
9761 Variel Avenue
Chatsworth, CA 91311

Steve Tague
239 Park Avenue South, #6D
New York, NY 10003

Tom Vack
Via Cascatti 25
I-22100 Cotco
Milan, Italy

Huyghe Veronique
48 Rue Saint Sabin
75011 Paris, France

Kenji Wakairo
1007, 9-5 Sarugakucho, Shibuyaku
Tokyo, 150, Japan

Stan Waldhauser
3220 Orchard Venue North
Golden Valley, MN 55422

William Whitehurst
256 Fifth Avenue
New York, NY 10010

Rick Whittey
Rick Whittey Photography
136 Simsbury Road
Avon, CT 06001

Kenneth Willardt
100W 23rd Street, 5th Floor
New York, NY 10011

C.J. Zablocki
VA Medical Center
5000 West National Avenue
Milwaukee, WI 53214

Index

DESIGNERS

238